A GUIDE TO THE
CHURCHES AND CHAPELS OF WALES

A GUIDE TO THE CHURCHES AND CHAPELS OF WALES

Edited by
JONATHAN M. WOODING
and
NIGEL YATES

UNIVERSITY OF WALES PRESS
CARDIFF
2011

www.uwp.co.uk

British Library Cataloguing-in-Publication Data
A catalogue record for this book is available from the British Library.

ISBN 978-0-7083-2118-8
e-ISBN 978-0-7083-2414-1

Printed by CPI Antony Rowe, Chippenham, Wiltshire

Contents

Illustrations

The picture section is placed between pages 164–5

Notes on Contributors

Peter Howell (PH) taught Classics in the University of London for thirty-five years. He is a former chairman of the Victorian Society, he served on the English Heritage Churches Committee and is a member of the Roman Catholic Historic Churches Committee for Wales and Herefordshire. In 2004 he reviewed the operation of the ecclesiastical exemption in Wales for the Welsh Assembly Government. He has written about Victorian churches and about Wales.

Prys Morgan (PM) is emeritus professor of history, Swansea University, and has written on many aspects of Welsh history. He was a member of the National Trust's Committee for Wales, a member of the Historic Buildings Council for Wales (Cadw) and is a member of the listed buildings committee of the Wales Synod of the United Reformed Church. He is currently president of the Honourable Society of Cymmrodorion.

John Newman (JN) retired in 2001 as reader in the history of British architecture at the Courtauld Institute of Art, University of London. He wrote the volumes in the Pevsner Buildings of Wales series on *Glamorgan* (1995) and *Gwent/Monmouthshire* (2000). He is a member of the Royal Commission on the Ancient and Historical Monuments of Wales.

Adam Voelcker (AV) is an architect working from home in Gwynedd, in private practice with his wife Frances. Most of his work is involved with minor historic buildings, particularly churches. He is also a member of the Bangor Diocesan Advisory Committee (DAC). He is co-author of the last in the Pevsner Buildings of Wales series, on *Gwynedd* (2009).

Jonathan Wooding (JW) is senior lecturer and director of the Centre for the Study of Religion in Celtic Societies at University of Wales Trinity Saint David. He specialises in the study of the archaeology and history of the early church in Britain and Ireland. He has published widely on medieval settlement history and on the cult of saints. He advises on tourist information and guiding for Welsh churches.

Nigel Yates (NY) was professor of ecclesiastical history at the University of Wales Lampeter (now Trinity Saint David), where he taught a module on Christian worship and church buildings. Between 1981 and 1991 he was an expert member of the Executive Committee of the Council for the Care of Churches, giving evidence at a number of consistory court hearings into liturgical reordering. He published widely on church furnishings and liturgical arrangement in the post-Reformation period and in 2008 completed a new book on Scottish church interiors since 1560. He died in January 2009.

The entry for the Greek Orthodox Church of St Nicholas in Cardiff has been contributed by Dr Andreas Andreopoulos (AA), lecturer in Orthodox theology at the University of Winchester.

Guide to Entries

All entries in the six sections of the guide that follow are arranged in a standard format.

(1) The name of the place, normally in the Welsh form approved by the (now defunct) Board of Celtic Studies. In certain cases where the English variant of the name is in common usage that form has been preferred. In the case of places with both English and Welsh names, both have been used, for example, Brecon/Aberhonddu.

(2) The title and denomination of the church or chapel. In the case of buildings no longer in use for worship, the original denomination has been given, followed by the present ownership or custodial arrangements.

(3) The local authority within which the building is situated according to the following code:

Mid Wales	Cere.	Ceredigion
	Powys (B)	Powys (pre-1974 Breconshire)
	Powys (D)	Powys (pre-1974 Denbighshire)
	Powys (M)	Powys (pre-1974 Montgomeryshire)
	Powys (R)	Powys (pre-1974 Radnorshire)
North-east Wales	Denb.	Denbighshire
	Flint.	Flintshire
	Wrex.	Wrexham
North-west Wales	Angl.	Anglesey
	Conwy	Conwy
	Gwyn. (C)	Gwynedd (pre-1974 Caernarfonshire)
	Gwyn. (M)	Gwynedd (pre-1974 Merionethshire)

South Wales	*Bridg.*	Bridgend
	Cardiff	Cardiff
	Merthyr	Merthyr Tydfil
	Neath PT	Neath Port Talbot
	Rhondda	Rhondda Cynon Taff
	Vale Glam.	Vale of Glamorgan
South-east Wales	*Mons*	Monmouthshire
	Newpt	Newport
	Torfaen	Torfaen
South-west Wales	*Carms*	Carmarthenshire
	Pembs	Pembrokeshire
	Swan.	Swansea

(4) The main entry text giving a brief description and evaluation of the building concluding with the initials of the contributor drafting the entry as listed in the notes on contributors.

(5) Details of location in relation to main roads and towns.

(6) Details of access. Where buildings are not open outside service times the times of services are given.

Although all details were correct at the time of going to press the editors cannot accept liability for their continuing accuracy as changes may have occurred in the meantime.

Introduction

The Church prior to the Reformation

Church organisation

The first Christians in Wales arrived during the period of Roman rule in Britain (AD 43–*c*.406). Wales was then a remote part of the – itself remote – Roman province of Britannia. Christianity would most likely have first arrived in Britain as the private faith of mobile individuals. We imagine that such early believers tended to congregate in towns more than in the countryside, though some country villas in England have been found to contain Christian mosaics and artefacts. This was not a world of public churches; worship was mostly outside the public gaze, in private houses and rooms, sometimes practised furtively on account of the periodic threat of imperial persecution. A strong tradition, found as early as the writings of Gildas in the sixth century, holds that Aaron and Iulius, two of Britain's early Christian martyrs, were martyred in Wales at the Roman town (*civitas*) at Caerleon (Newport), perhaps in the magnificent amphitheatre still visible there.

The Edict of Milan (313) and the subsequent conversion of Constantine (325) brought Christianity into a more central role in Roman society. How far Christianity penetrated the largely rural society of Wales under Roman rule remains controversial. Roman rule in Britain ended in the early 400s and Germanic settlers subsequently occupied most of what is now England. There the Romano-British church disappeared under the rule of non-Christian Anglo-Saxon kings, though it continued to exist in western Britain. The continuity of the post-Roman Welsh church with its Roman predecessor may possibly be seen in the proximity of early medieval monasteries to former Roman villas at Llantwit Major and at Llandough, near Penarth (Vale of Glamorgan).

Many of the older churches in Wales claim origins in the period, the early Middle Ages (*c.*400–1000), which immediately followed the Roman period. This is usually because the dedication of the church is to a saint whose career is traced to this period – popularly referred to as the 'Age of the Saints'. Often the dedication is embedded in an early medieval place name, such as *llan* + the name of the saint: Llangadog (church of St Cadog), or Llanbadarn ('church of St Padarn'). One should be wary of taking these dedications as definite evidence of foundation *by* the saints (who after all would not dedicate churches to themselves). There are cases where we can see that a site has come to be named after its incumbent or its owner, but dedications to saints very often have nothing to do with the presence of the saint him- or herself at the site, being simply evidence that the founder of a church was particularly devoted to the cult of a particular saint. Claims of early medieval origins for many Welsh churches are, however, likely to be correct, as the decline of Roman rule and the advent of monasticism, occurring in this period, almost certainly led to a reshaping of settlement patterns while Christianity established itself as the dominant faith of Wales. On many sites, burials and early Christian monuments (ECMs), in Latin or Ogham script, attest to an early medieval date.

In the decades leading up to the Roman withdrawal from Britain the Church began to establish an infrastructure for ministering to an increasing Christian population. Our written records of this process are limited to a few sources, almost all written outside Britain, although archaeology can add to their testimony. This was, broadly speaking, a church centred on the Roman political map. Bishops ministered to the people from bases in the main towns. The texts are mostly silent concerning the specific situation in Wales. The handful of demonstrably early written sources, such as the *Life* of the Welsh-born bishop of Dol in Brittany, St Samson, and the early charters in the Book of Llandaff, present a picture of a church evolving out of the Roman model. There were no parishes. Ordinary priests could be married and have families. Churches belonged to their own regions and states; bishops were more or less local appointments – a situation that changed only with the Gregorian Reform in the eleventh century. Bishops did consecrate other bishops, and rulings of councils of bishops constituted a body of canon law separate from everyday law, but the idea of the Church as a structure separate from the state was at best embryonic.

Churchyards and church buildings were not separately the property of the Church as a corporation, and could be owned by private persons or lords.

In early medieval Wales priests might be found in monasteries and in private churches, with parishes not introduced until the arrival of the Normans. Dioceses are often assumed to have been coterminous with kingdoms but, in the *Life of St Samson*, the bishop Dubricius (St Dyfrig) appears to exercise authority across more than one kingdom. When Asser (d.908), the biographer of King Alfred, and a member of the episcopal family of St Davids, describes his native diocese he speaks of the *monasterium et parochia Sancti Degui*. The bishop, Asser's kinsman, thus ministers from a *monasterium* – probably a 'mother church' of monastic origin and collegiate character – over a territory defined by the sphere of influence of the saint's community. A text known as the 'Seven Bishop Houses of Dyfed' further suggests that around the ninth century each constituent *cantref* of Dyfed had its own local bishop. These are the barest glimpses of an evolving pattern across a millennium.

As the first millennium drew to a close, communities of non-celibate priests (*claswyr*) are seen ministering to large territories, working out of mother-churches (*clasau*). Some of the larger churches with *clas* communities, such as Clynnog Fawr (Gwynedd) and Llanbadarn Fawr (Ceredigion), although the present structures date from after the *clas* period, reflect in their size and decoration a status second only to cathedrals in this pattern of organisation. The *clas* seems to have been in origin a monastic community, with the inherited abbacy later often held by a layman or secular priest. It is perhaps inevitable that this development would come to be condemned by later writers as a corruption of the monastic ideal. Gerald of Wales was incensed at the idea of a titular abbot bearing a spear, but such scenes were, it must be said, consistent with the mentality of the armed crusade that Gerald had himself come to preach. The *clas* was a dynamic response to the particular circumstances of the time and place. It is in the former *clas* churches that some of our richest medieval architectural remains are to be found. Liturgical change has often seen such churches stripped of transepts, screens and other medieval features, but medieval windows, vaults, arches, fonts and ornamentation dating from the eleventh through to the thirteenth centuries are still to be seen in many churches.

There were also monasteries that explored the more traditionally austere side of monasticism. The first monastic impulses had arrived from Gaul in the fifth or sixth century and writings by the British churchmen Gildas and Finnian provide glimpses of the spirituality of sixth-century monastic founders such as St Illtud of Llantwit Major and the more ascetic St David, a spirituality that also inspired monastic leaders in Ireland. While the *clasau* came to replace older monastic foundations, the contemplative life had a resurgence in the second millennium. Eremitical communities (*colidei*) are identified at Bardsey (Ynys Enlli) and Beddgelert by Gerald of Wales in the twelfth century, around the same time that continental impulses for monastic reform began to penetrate Wales. The Augustinian Canons, following a rule attributed to St Augustine, formed a new body of churches with celibate canons, but providing team ministries from a central church in some ways comparable to the *clasau*, and taking over some *clas* churches.

From the late eleventh century onwards these new monastic impulses were joined by the reformed Benedictine orders. These orders had their genesis in the Cluniac order (founded in 909) in France, though the Cistercian order (founded 1098) would have the greater impact in Wales. When the reformed Benedictine orders first came into south Wales, under the influence of Norman settlement, their failure to achieve abbey status in many cases meant that these 'alien priories' were isolated and lacking in influence. The Cistercians, by contrast, founded fourteen abbeys and came to control thousands of acres of Welsh farmland, enjoying patronage of both the Norman settlers and the native princes. Their intensive methods of agriculture, developed in France and brought to Wales, shaped the Welsh uplands as well as contributing the grand abbey buildings that mostly now stand ruined in the Welsh landscape.

Though these 'foreign' orders are often typically contrasted in popular works with the 'native' Celtic monasteries, patronage of the Cistercians by the Welsh princes arguably made them as 'Celtic' as their predecessors. The monastery of Strata Florida (Ceredigion), the most important Cistercian foundation in Wales, was founded under the patronage of the native ruler Rhys ap Gruffydd of Deheubarth (d.1197). It was at times a meeting place for government, the burial place of rulers (it is sometimes described as the 'Westminster Abbey of Wales'), and was the place at which the 'Chronicle of the Princes' (*Brut y Tywysogion*) was written, amongst other works of Welsh literature.

The Welsh Church came in time more or less completely to adopt the same territorial model as had emerged in England. The older, possibly non-territorial, episcopates such as Cynidr and Llandeilo Fawr disappeared around the end of the first millennium, to be replaced by the four territorial bishoprics of St Davids, Bangor, Llandaff and St Asaph. At least two of these, Bangor and St Davids, were based on dioceses of a much earlier date, so the new organisation must be understood as being as much a development out of native institutions as an imposition by Norman invaders. The *clasau* gradually declined in significance and the *clas* churches were in time mostly reduced to the status of parish churches, or in some cases were absorbed into the new collegiate structures of cathedral chapters and the religious canonries of the Augustinians. The *clas* at St Davids was turned into a college of secular canons by Bishop Bernard (1115–48) and four archdeaconries were established. In the late twelfth century prebendaries were created. Similar patterns were followed in the dioceses of Bangor, Llandaff and St Asaph in the thirteenth century.

Church buildings from late antiquity to the end of the Middle Ages

We can presume, on analogy with other parts of the empire, that the first church buildings in Britain were former public meeting houses and other Roman civic structures, which in time became dedicated church buildings and chapels. The dead, according to Roman custom, were mostly buried outside town walls in 'extramural' cemeteries, which themselves sometimes became the sites of churches commemorating the earliest Christians – in the same way as the early churches on the Appian Way in Rome began. The burial monument of the sixth-century man named Carausius, now in the parish church of Penmachno (Gwynedd), states that he lies 'in this heap of stones' (*hoc congeries lapidum*). This short inscription evokes a world in which monuments to the earliest Christians were visible in the wider landscape, by roads and in fields, as well as at sites of formal worship.

Monasticism had inspired a conscious retreat from the settled world into empty places (*deserta*) analogous with the eastern desert fathers, creating further Christian churches and monuments in the rural landscape. Although these were conceptually 'outside' the everyday secular world, monastic churches, in colonising the emptier and remoter parts of the landscape, brought the possibility of pastoral care to a wider range of people than before. The location of the cathedral at St Davids, almost hidden in the bottom of a deep, damp valley, is a product of its monastic origin. The removal of the bishop's palace from St Davids to Carmarthen in the later Middle Ages was a response to the tension between the historic origins of the site and the changing needs of the diocese. In Llandaff the medieval episcopal seat in the countryside came to be absorbed into the suburban development of the modern city of Cardiff.

Churches thus can have their origins, variously, in 'secular' churches attached to early settlements, monastic churches founded away from settlements, and mortuary chapels. Nothing much survives of the church buildings of the late Roman and early medieval period. Place names, early monuments, sometimes the very shape of the site itself, may be of early medieval origins but, with the exception of some culturally Anglo-Saxon masonry at Presteigne (Powys), no standing church building in Wales can be confidently dated much before the year 1100. The earliest buildings, whether of wood or of stone, have not survived the demand for frequent and wholesale rebuilding to accommodate a living and growing faith which periodically reshaped its ideas of liturgy and worship.

What then can we see of these different communities of Christians in our church sites today? The setting and form of the site itself may be artefacts of early date. One early artefact may be the name of the site. The world *llan*, prefixed to another name, very often indicates a first-millennium date (though antiquarian examples, or 'back-formations', of such names can occur). The Welsh name of the village of Llanilltud Fawr (English: Llanwit Major) means 'the great church of Illtud' and commemorates St Illtud, a monastic leader of the sixth century who probably did indeed live at the site. Where a saint's name occurs with *llan*, however, it is as likely that the church is a foundation by 'cult' venerators of the saint after the time of the saint him- or herself, especially if the saint in question is well known. Hence the many Llanddewi churches are likely to reflect the later spread of influence of the church at St Davids, rather than the travels of Dewi Sant himself. Most of the *llan-* names themselves are likely to be early in date, if not coincident with the initial foundation, but the names doubtless mask layers of history. At Llanllŷr (Ceredigion) an ECM (in private hands) shows the ownership of the site by the cult of a different saint (Modomnóc) to the saint (Llŷr) named in the place name, and, moreover, records that the site was earlier named after a third person, the hermit Ditóc.

ECMs will be the earliest structures on many church sites. From at least the sixth century onwards early Christians in Wales were commemorated with stones inscribed in either the Roman script (broadly the same as our alphabet) or in the Ogham script (a cipher based on lines cut on the edge of a stone and used to write the Irish language). These tend to be memorials to named individuals and, depending on the history of the site being visited, may commemorate abbots, benefactors, proprietors or prominent *claswyr*. Although these are found now inside buildings – often built into walls of churches, or functioning as window sills or lintels – it is clear that most once were standing pillars in churchyards, where many are known to have stood within living memory, or as recorded in pictorial or written record. These stones are amongst our best evidence for early Christianity in Wales. The use of formulaic phrases such as HIC IACIT (*hic iacet*: 'here lies') indicates the origins of this type of monument in Roman models of commemoration. The earliest stones show mainly familial or regional affiliations, but a movement towards more overtly Christian formulae is seen around the seventh and eighth centuries. This, along with the emergence of *llan* names around the same period, may mark a new focus of burial on now established Christian sites with churchyards: one meaning of *llan* is 'enclosure'. The Ogham stones are regional groups, confined to the very south-west (the early medieval kingdom of Dyfed), around Brecon (the early medieval kingdom of Brycheiniog) and in Gwynedd. These distributions correspond to early Irish political groups living in Wales, and are very likely to reflect monuments to early Irish Christians.

The predominant building method of the early Middle Ages was in wood. The proliferation of stone churches dates from the eleventh and twelfth centuries, with Gruffydd ap Cynan (d.1137) recorded as a prolific builders of churches – his Welsh biographer describes Gwynedd in his day as 'bespangled with lime-washed churches as the firmament is with stars'. The very large number of church buildings, around nine hundred in total, which date from the second half of the Middle Ages is the product of a variety of cultural influences and pastoral models. The typical ground plans of these churches fall into three key categories: cruciform, twin cell and single cell. Attempts have been made to assign these ground plans to the taxonomy of 'mother' and 'local' churches, but it is clear that this is not a simple matter. We cannot determine in all cases if extensions of simpler buildings reflect real need for space or simply the degree of patronage of the church. Certainly, many churches that are in origin *clas* churches are cruciform in plan, such as Clynnog Fawr (Gwynedd), Llanbadarn Fawr and Llanddewi Brefi (Ceredigion). Other *clas* churches, such as Aberdaron and Llancarfan, are twin-nave structures. Some of these churches attained their present extent only after the *clas* period, however; changing patronage and growth in pilgrimage in the period around 1500 accounts for the present scale and quality of churches such as Beaumaris, Clynnog Fawr, Holyhead and Llanelian. The expansion in size of many churches was also a response to liturgical change. Increase in the practice of burial inside churches led to the widening of aisles, and liturgical change, beginning in the later first millennium, saw the gradual addition of side altars at which private devotions could take place or masses held separately from the main altar. Large and elaborate fonts are a regular survival from this period. As churches increased in size and complexity there was increased division of the interior spaces by screens, with the nave becoming not just a place for communal worship but, in the larger churches, a place for non-ecclesiastical meetings and even for the transaction of commerce.

The dissolution of the monasteries in the 1530s under Henry VIII saw most of the monastic communities broken up and their possessions confiscated. The size and character of the Cistercian buildings meant that few of them would be reused as parish churches, though the church at Margam (Neath PT) is one example where this has happened. However, through the reuse of some Benedictine buildings, for example, at Ewenny (Vale of Glamorgan), we can experience the flavour of the monastic as opposed to the secular architectural vision, with its limited use of windows and clear division of internal space preserved even through much alteration. These are reminders of how our medieval church sites, although often similar to the eye today, are of diverse origins.

Towards the end of the Middle Ages, in the richer or more anglicised parts of Wales, very large churches, comparable with those in England, began to be built. There are good examples in Mid Wales at Guilsfield, Montgomery, Old Radnor and Presteigne, the last two being ecclesiastically part of the English diocese of Hereford; in the north-east at Denbigh, Gresford, Holt and Wrexham; in the north-west at Conwy; and in the south at Abergavenny, Cardiff (St John's), Carmarthen, Grosmont, Haverfordwest (St Mary's), Laugharne, Magor, Skenfrith and Tenby. These were all either places near the border with England or towns in which English influence was strong. In the rest of Wales the building of churches that were relatively small, though frequently rich in terms of architectural detail, continued through to the Reformation and beyond.

The post-Reformation churches in Wales

The Reformation which swept across Europe from the 1520s transformed the religious landscape of Wales, though the precise nature of its operation was almost entirely determined by political events in England. The Welsh monasteries were the first casualty, all dissolved and their estates sold off in the late 1530s. This had a profound effect on the parishes as many had been appropriated to the monasteries which had either served them personally or appointed vicars to do so. Their patronage and, in many cases, the bulk of the parochial income fell into lay hands and this accounted for their subsequent poverty in the post-Reformation period. Although Wales was, like the northern and western parts of England, religiously conservative, it had one of the earliest reform-minded bishops in the notoriously unpopular William Barlow of St Davids (1536–48) and there were no disturbances in Wales, as there were in Cornwall, when the first English prayer book was introduced in 1549, even though the new services must have been as unintelligible to the Welsh-speaking population as the Latin services that preceded them, and without the latter's familiarity. There is, however, some evidence that there was considerable support in Wales for the temporary restoration of

Roman Catholicism under Queen Mary (1553–8). However, one of the Welsh bishops, Anthony Kitchin of Llandaff (1545–63), was the only bishop in England and Wales to take the oath to Queen Elizabeth and thereby acquiesce, admittedly rather passively, in the Protestant religious settlement of 1559, and this settlement was successful in Wales whereas it was not so in Ireland. The reasons for this were twofold: the first was the appointment of exceptionally able men as the first Protestant bishops, notably Richard Davies of St Davids (1561–81) who was instrumental in ensuring that the Welsh Church was provided with its own translation of the Bible and Book of Common Prayer. The second was the popularity of these new texts in the native language. The prayer book and New Testament in Welsh were published in 1567 and the complete Bible in 1588.

As a result, most of the parishes in Wales seem to have been fully conforming to the new Protestant church by the 1570s, although the widespread survival of rood screens, and some rood lofts, in parts of Wales suggests that there was an enduring conservatism among both clergy and laity, seen in a reluctance to dispose of traditional church furnishings. There was also a strong survival of popular religious customs, such as ceremonies attached to funerals, recourse to holy wells and the continuance of certain liturgical traditions such *Mabsant* and *Plygain*. These, however, did not indicate any lack of support for the established church which, even in the new high-church Anglican outlook it adopted in the 1620s, was able to count on the loyalty of the vast majority of the population of Wales. Two of the finest examples of high-church Anglican architecture of the seventeenth century survive in the private chapels at Gwydir Uchaf and Rûg. Surviving Roman Catholic families were very small in numbers and largely confined to the border counties of Flintshire and Monmouthshire. Protestant dissent from the Anglican Church, in the form of Baptists, Independents, Presbyterians and Quakers, was no stronger in Wales, and if anything slightly weaker, than it was in England in the late seventeenth century. During the early years of the eighteenth century, Protestant dissent in Wales was further weakened when a number of Independent and Presbyterian congregations became Unitarian rather than Trinitarian in doctrine. Unitarian congregations were, and still are, particularly strong along the Teifi valley in northern Carmarthenshire and southern Ceredigion.

The growth of Nonconformity in Wales, which was such an important feature of the principality by the middle years of the nineteenth century, was almost entirely the result of the Evangelical revival within the Anglican Church, which began in Wales in the 1730s with the preaching of Howel Harris and Daniel Rowland. By the 1760s, there were flourishing communities of Evangelicals throughout south Wales, many of which had built their own chapels. They did not regard themselves as separatists but merely as 'societies' within the Anglican Church. Their leaders were mostly Anglican clergy although they permitted laymen to preach in their own chapels. They continued to attend services and the sacrament of Holy Communion in their parish churches but used their own chapels for more informal services, which involved much hymn singing, of a type not provided by the Book of Common Prayer. The attitude of the Anglican bishops and clergy towards these new Evangelical groups, generally known as Methodists, varied. Some clergy openly supported them and even some bishops such as Richard Watson of Llandaff (1782–1816) and Thomas Burgess of St Davids (1803–25) were not unsympathetic. Others, however, saw the Methodists as undisciplined, potentially heretical and politically radical, and, by the 1790s, with the outbreak of revolution and extreme anti-clericalism in France, this was the majority position within the Anglican Church. There is, however, no doubt that Methodism had an enormous attraction, particularly the hymn singing and emotional preaching, for many ordinary people in Wales. From the 1780s, under the leadership of Thomas Charles of Bala, an Anglican clergyman, Methodism became as strong in north Wales as it had become in south Wales a generation earlier. Pressure on Charles from Methodists who were enraged by the attacks on them from Anglican bishops and clergy eventually led to his agreeing, very reluctantly in 1811, to the ordination of some of the lay preachers so that they could celebrate Holy Communion in their own chapels. This was the beginning of the formal schism that resulted in the setting up of the Presbyterian Church of Wales a decade later.

Even before this individual Methodist congregations had seceded from the Anglican Church to join one of the older Nonconformist bodies, so that the Evangelical Revival in Wales did not just create a new denomination and a severe weakening of the Anglican Church, but also led to a strengthening of the older Nonconformist bodies. By the religious census of 1851, only one in five people worshipping regularly every Sunday in Wales were to be found in an Anglican church; of the remainder, the vast majority belonged to the Presbyterian Church of Wales (also known as the Calvinistic Methodists), the Baptists or the Independents. The Wesleyan Methodists, strong in some parts of England, were weak in Wales. Roman Catholics remained virtually non-existent.

Both Nonconformists, and later even Anglicans, blamed the collapse of Anglicanism in Wales on the 'corruptions' of the established church and, in particular, the fact that since the 1720s Wales had had no native-born Welsh-speaking Anglican bishops. Recent research is beginning to show that this interpretation of Welsh religious history, repeated uncritically for more than a hundred years, is simply not true. The evidence from visitation returns and other sources shows that the condition of Anglican religion in Wales in the eighteenth and early nineteenth centuries was extremely strong. Even if bishops did not themselves speak Welsh, and several learned enough to be able to confirm in Welsh, they generally insisted that clergy were Welsh speaking in those parishes where the majority of the population did not speak English. Services were regular and churches generally well maintained. The significant number of unaltered late eighteenth- or early nineteenth-century church interiors in Wales, especially in the diocese of Bangor (for example, Llanfaglan, Llangwyllog and Ynyscynhaearn), bears witness to a substantial amount of church building and restoration in this period. In Wales a significant number of rural churches had a monthly celebration of Holy Communion, whereas in England this was largely confined to the towns and the norm in the villages was three or four times a year. Another illustration of the effectiveness of Anglicanism in the eighteenth century was the extensive provision for elementary education, in the form of either charity schools or the circulating schools established in south-west Wales by Griffith Jones of Llanddowror and continued after his death by Bridget Bevan of Laugharne. By the early nineteenth century most Welsh bishops were enthusiastic supporters of the National Society for the Education of the Poor established in 1811. In the diocese of St Davids, Bishop Burgess made provision for the education of his clergy, who could not afford to attend Oxford or Cambridge, with the establishment of St David's College at Lampeter; the foundation stone was laid in 1822 and the first students admitted in 1827.

The strength of Nonconformity in Wales in the nineteenth century has resulted in a somewhat poor survival of early buildings and even fewer with unaltered interiors, though there are outstanding examples at Capel Newydd at Nanhoron, Yr Hen Fethel at Garnant, the Pales Meeting House at Llandegley and Capel Penrhiw, re-erected at the Museum of Welsh National History in St Fagans. Many early chapels were either completely rebuilt or at least extensively refurnished by congregations now sufficiently wealthy to find the simple meeting houses of their forbears insufficient for their improved social status. Far more typical are the expensive late nineteenth-century chapels with their handsome porticos and their lavish internal woodwork though the rate of closure, resulting in either demolition or redevelopment, in recent years has been alarming and greatly damaging to the architectural heritage of Wales. The 1851 religious census seems to have been the high watermark for Nonconformity in Wales. Fifty years later it was already in decline and Anglicanism had begun to recover. During the twentieth century Nonconformity declined even more rapidly, overtaken not just by Anglicanism but by a newly resurgent Roman Catholicism under the leadership of Archbishops Francis Edward Mostyn and Michael Joseph McGrath.

Anglicanism in Wales, as in England, was revitalised in the second half of the nineteenth century both by those Evangelicals who had remained within the established church and a new breed of high churchmen who were disciples of the Oxford Movement. Both groups were less successful initially in Wales than they were in England but they had begun to make a mark by the end of the century. Two of the earliest Anglican religious communities for men were established in Wales, by Father Ignatius at Llanthony and by Dom Aelred Carlyle on the island of Caldey. By that time, however, what dominated Anglicanism in Wales was the struggle over the proposed disestablishment of the Anglican Church. This had long been part of the programme of the dominant Liberal Party in Wales but it was rather lower down the English Liberal agenda and it was not until the Liberal landslide of 1906, and the loss of every Conservative seat in Wales, that it became official government policy. Whereas the disestablishment of the Church of Ireland in 1869 had been difficult to oppose, since it counted on the support of such a small minority of the population, Anglicans in Wales could point to an increase in support for them since the disastrous figures of the 1851 religious census. From the 1830s there had been pressure from some Anglicans in Wales for the appointment of native-born, Welsh-speaking bishops, and this had eventually been conceded in 1870 with the appointment of Joshua Hughes to St Asaph. His successor there, Alfred George Edwards (1889–1934), and Bishop John Owen of St Davids (1897–1926) led the opposition to the Welsh Disestablishment Bill but eventually had to concede defeat and an independent Church in Wales was formed in 1920 with Edwards as its first archbishop. A few parishes in Powys along the border with England remained in the English diocese of Hereford.

The programmes of church building and restoration that dominated the religious life of England in the second half of the nineteenth century were replicated in Wales. In addition to the programme of Nonconformist chapel building and refurbishment, many Anglican churches were rebuilt or restored and new buildings were erected for the growing urban communities in north-east and south-east Wales. The poverty of the Welsh Anglican Church meant, however, that there were fewer churches by major Victorian architects, though some examples of work by all the major figures of the period – Pearson, Scott, Street and others – can still be found, and some of these, such as the early Tractarian church at Llangasty Talyllyn or the Arts and Crafts church at Brithdir, are of outstanding quality. Many Welsh rural churches, especially in the south-west, were, however, cheaply replaced or restored by local architects. One particularly interesting feature of the conservatism of Welsh Anglicanism in this period was the patchy nature of the ecclesiological movement in Wales before the last quarter of the nineteenth century. Whereas in England churches were reordered from the 1840s in a neo-medievalist manner, with box pews replaced by open benches, the replacement of three- or two-decker pulpits by separate pulpits and lecterns and the removal of the choir from a west gallery in the nave to stalls in the chancel; in Wales the buildings tended to be neo-medievalist in terms of their fabrics, but largely pre-ecclesiological in terms of their furnishings and liturgical arrangement. There are good examples of such buildings from the 1850s and 1860s at Leighton, Llandwrog, Llanigon, Llanfyllin and

Llangwyfan. In this respect, Wales was lagging roughly twenty to thirty years behind England. The slow growth of Roman Catholicism in the second half of the nineteenth century, not assisted by the fact that the first Welsh diocese, Newport and Menevia, had its episcopal headquarters in Herefordshire at the cathedral monastery of Belmont, also meant that there are relatively few major buildings from this period. By contrast, the more rapid growth of Roman Catholicism in the twentieth century, following the establishment of the new archdiocese of Cardiff in 1916, has resulted in the building of a few interesting modern churches, such as the church in Amlwch and the shrine of Our Lady of the Taper in Cardigan, compared with the relative paucity of such work for the other religious denominations in Wales.

Aims of the present guide

This guide aims to include as representative a selection as possible of the churches and chapels in Wales which show work of importance from the earliest days of Welsh Christianity to the present day. Inevitably, the majority belong to the Church in Wales as it retains the vast majority of medieval buildings. In the case of post-Reformation churches and chapels we have tried to include a fair denominational as well as geographical balance. We have, however, included only those buildings to which there is reasonable access as there is nothing more frustrating than travelling many miles to see a building which turns out to be locked and where there is no information as to when it is open or where to find the key. Unfortunately, there are a number of significant buildings which really had to be included where access is difficult outside service times and we have, in these cases, given details of Sunday or weekday services. Nevertheless, it is our hope that the increase of church tourism in Wales will encourage the development in the principality of the sort of Open Churches scheme that has operated very successfully in Scotland for several years. Where churches and chapels are no longer in use as places of worship they are included where they have been transferred to bodies such as the Friends of Friendless Churches or local trusts, and are still accessible, but not where they have been effectively abandoned or so heavily adapted for non-ecclesiastical use that most of their furnishings have been removed.

In bringing the contents of this guide together we have not sought to impose either a uniform word length or a rigid house style on contributors. The selection of a particular church or chapel has been the result of discussion between the contributors but still retains a large element of personal choice, and this is reflected in the style and content of the entries, some of which will concentrate on fabric rather than furnishings or vice versa. We do, however, believe that the final selection is a balanced one, with entries for churches in virtually every part of Wales and with a substantial number of non-Anglican buildings being included in the selection of post-Reformation churches. The aim of the guide is to encourage the reader to visit and appreciate these buildings and to make churches and chapels a more significant element in determining the future direction of both the heritage and tourism policies of public bodies in Wales.

Jonathan Wooding
Nigel Yates
University of Wales Trinity St David

Acknowledgements

The editors would like to thank their fellow contributors – Peter Howell, Prys Morgan, John Newman and Adam Voelcker – for their valuable contributions to this guide, and to Adam Voelcker for providing some of the illustrations. They would also like to thank Laura Jarvis, in the Department of Theology and Religious Studies at the University of Wales Trinity St David, who did the bulk of the work of coordinating the various parts of the text, checking on access arrangements and scanning the illustrations. Without her help the production of this guide would not have been possible.

Additional note

My co-editor Nigel Yates passed away on 15 January 2009, while this book was in the last stages of editing. With his untimely death Wales has lost one of its foremost church historians; we at Trinity Saint David have lost an irreplaceable, inspirational colleague and friend. Visiting the churches of Wales, large and small, was very dear to Nigel's heart and I hope that through this volume readers will come to love these buildings as he did. I would like to thank, in particular, Adam Voelcker for his advice on several points, Martin Crampin, John Morgan-Guy and Laura Jarvis for help in choosing illustrations in the absence of Nigel's comprehensive knowledge of interiors.

Jonathan Wooding

1

Churches and Chapels in Mid Wales

1. ABBEY CWMHIR (St Mary), Church in Wales   *Powys (R)*

Location: off the A483, 7 miles north of Llandrindod Wells.
Access: generally open.

Cistercian abbey in this remote valley, founded in 1143, which had the largest church in Wales, now almost completely destroyed. The old estate of the Fowlers passed in the mid-nineteenth century to the Phillips family of Manchester, and it was Miss Phillips who paid for the new church built in 1866–7. The architects were John Wilkes Poundley, surveyor of Montgomeryshire, and David Walker of Birkenhead. It has all the character one would expect from them. It is of knobbly brownish stone, in Early French Gothic style. The porch is within a tower which turns broached, and then into an octagonal spirelet, with a ring of colonnettes between. The relief of the Ascension over the door is copied from a tympanum which may have come from the abbey. The east window has a gable over it, interrupting the apsidal chancel roof. Within, the chancel arch, pulpit and font are richly carved. Especially wonderful is the glass in the apse windows, by Heaton, Butler and Bayne, to the design of Robert Turnill Bayne (1866). It is of Pre-Raphaelite intensity, with rich browns, greens and purples. The scene of Christ's Agony in the Garden is particularly fine. The glass in the west window is by Clayton and Bell. Poundley and Walker also designed the Hall, built in 1867, gabled and bargeboarded, with a striped slate roof. The diarist Francis Kilvert much admired it.

PH

2. ABEREDW (St Cewydd), Church in Wales   *Powys (R)*

Location: in village, on the west side of the B4567, 3 miles south-east of Builth Wells.

Access: key holder advertised on notice board.

A large, late medieval church, with a west tower and a handsome north porch. Both nave and chancel roofs are medieval, that of the chancel being ceiled in a style more familiar in south-west England. Nave and chancel are separated by a screen, the lower part of which dates from the fifteenth century and the upper part from the seventeenth century. The wrought iron altar rails date from the early nineteenth century. An unusual survival is two flutes and a pitch pipe that belonged to the musicians who accompanied the church choir before the installation of the organ.

NY

3. BEULAH (Eglwys Oen Duw – Church of the Lamb of God), Church in Wales   *Powys (R)*

Location: off the A483, 1 mile north of Beulah.

Access: generally open.

In such a remote location, one is surprised to find this strikingly elaborate Victorian church, in blue and grey stone, with a tall Germanic fleche. It was built by the Thomas family of Llwyn Madoc. The architect was John Norton. The exterior is in plain Early English, but the interior is colourful, with polychrome brick, tiles and a mosaic reredos. There is good Clayton and Bell glass in the grouped lancets of east and west windows, and two sanctuary windows are by Burlison and Grylls (*c*.1877). The pulpit is of wrought iron, the choir stalls are carved and there are brass candelabra. Note the brass sconces in the form of water lilies, complete with frogs. There are three fonts, one by Norton, and two early medieval ones from demolished churches.

PH

4. BLEDDFA (St Mary Magdalene), Church in Wales   *Powys (R)*

Location: on main road A488 to Llandrindod Wells, 5 miles south-west of Knighton.
Access: generally open.

The church comprises a single-cell nave and chancel of *c.*1400 with an eighteenth-century south porch and a simple wooden belfry at the west end of the nave, which was partitioned off in *c.*1800 to serve as a schoolroom. The interior is covered by a fifteenth-century roof. The pulpit and altar rails date from the seventeenth century. The church was attractively restored in 1977 by G. G. Pace, according to a scheme which allowed the furnishings to be moveable, so that the church could be used for concerts and exhibitions.

NY

5. BRECON/ABERHONDDU (Cathedral of St John the Evangelist), Church in Wales   *Powys (B)*

Location: on the west side of town above the River Honddu near the ruins of the former castle, now mostly incorporated into the Castle Hotel.
Access: open daily 9 a.m.–5.30 p.m.

This large cruciform former priory church, dating from the thirteenth and fourteenth centuries, was made the cathedral of the new diocese of Swansea and Brecon at its creation in 1923. An extensive restoration of the interior had been carried out by George Gilbert Scott between 1861 and 1875, and a further restoration, designed to make the building work as a cathedral, was carried out by W. D. Caröe in 1927–37. The very attractive interior is dominated by an east window of five lancets. There is a particularly handsome twelfth-century font and an even more handsome thirteenth-century sedilia and triple piscina. Most of the present furnishings are by either Scott or Caröe, those of the latter being the more successful. They include the magnificent new reredos to the high altar, designed to replicate a reredos of *c.*1500, filled with statuary. The chapel of St Keyne is separated from the nave by an early sixteenth-century parclose screen, to which have been attached bosses from the former choir ceiling. The former north transeptal chapels were in 1923 adapted to serve as the regimental chapel of the South Wales Borderers. In the south transept is a seventeenth-century cupboard incorporating carved panels of c.1500 said to have come from Neath Abbey. Parts of a fifteenth-century screen have also been incorporated into the pulpit.

The overall atmosphere of the cathedral is one of great spaciousness and liturgical formality. Substantial remains of the former priory buildings also remain incorporated into the largely nineteenth-century deanery and canonry houses. The former tithe barn has been converted to serve as a shop, exhibition area and restaurant, designed to meet the needs of visitors to the cathedral.

NY

6. CAPEL-Y-FFIN (St Mary), Church in Wales   *Powys (B)*

Location: on a side road to Llanthony, 6 miles south of Hay-on-Wye.
Access: generally open.

An extremely modest chapel-of-ease built in 1762 and with a south porch added in 1817. The furnishings are largely contemporary and comprise a simple pulpit of 1780, domestic settles instead of pews, altar rails and a gallery along the north wall reached by a staircase at the west end. There is a crude medieval font of uncertain date. The interior was insensitively carpeted, covering the stone flags, in 1991. Nearby is the former Anglican monastery (now a private house) designed by Charles Buckeridge for Father Ignatius of Llanthony in the 1870s and later occupied by the artists Eric Gill and David Jones.

NY

7. CARDIGAN/ABERTEIFI (Our Lady of the Taper), Roman Catholic

Cere.

Location: in the northern suburbs of Cardigan, on the main Aberystwyth road.

Access: generally open.

The church, with its attached free-standing shrine housing a miraculous statue of Our Lady, is an impressive piece of modern architecture designed by Weightman and Bullen of Liverpool in 1970 to provide a worthy setting for the new liturgy authorised by the Second Vatican Council. The furnishings and stained glass are of good quality with a spacious sanctuary being located under a funnel-like tower. The complex includes an attached presbytery and is one of very few examples of modern church architecture in rural Wales.

NY

8. CARNO (St John the Baptist), Church in Wales   *Powys (M)*

Location: in village, on the A470, midway between Newtown and Machynlleth.

Access: key available from the Post Office.

Opposite the Aleppo Merchant inn, on the road from Newtown to Machynlleth, is the characterful church of 1863 by J. W. Poundley and David Walker. It replaced a medieval church of which bits survive. It is a rich example of the architects' work, and it is tragic that the funny wooden belfry, painted maroon, has been removed from the amazing little tower, which, like the rest of the church, is of lumpy grey stone with red and yellow dressings. The windows have striking plate tracery. The division between nave and chancel is marked on the outside by frilly ironwork, and on the inside by a big timber arch resting on pairs of colonnettes.

PH

9. CASCOB (St Michael), Church in Wales   *Powys (R)*

Location: by itself on a side road off the B4357, 4 miles west of
Presteigne.
Access: generally open.

A small, largely fourteenth-century church, with a west tower and
timber belfry, typical of Powys. The church underwent a model
restoration in 1878 in which the fourteenth-century octagonal font, the
fifteenth-century roof and the early sixteenth-century screen, with the
panelled parapet of the rood loft still *in situ*, were retained. There is a
memorial to a former long-serving incumbent, William Jenkins Rees, the
distinguished Celtic scholar, who died in 1855.

NY

10. CREGRINA (St David), Church in Wales   *Powys (R)*

Location: on a side road off the A481, 4 miles east of Builth Wells.
Access: generally open.

The church comprises a thirteenth-century nave and a wider fifteenth-
century chancel, set at an angle to it, both of which were sensitively
restored in 1903. Nave and chancel are separated by a simple sixteenth-
century screen. The crude font is probably of the twelfth century.
The chancel was repaired by G. G. Pace in 1958 and the external walls
white-washed.

NY

11. DISSERTH (St Cewydd), Church in Wales   *Powys (R)*

Location: on a side road between the A483 and the B4358, 2 miles
south-west of Llandrindod Wells.
Access: generally open.

The church comprises a single-cell broad nave and chancel of the
fifteenth century with a west tower. Its external walls are whitewashed
and it retains one of the most complete late seventeenth- and early

eighteenth-century interiors in Wales. The three-decker pulpit, dated 1687, is placed in the middle of the south wall, with an open space to the east of it. The box pews, erected by the owners of the various properties in the parish and dated between 1666 and 1722, are arranged higgledy-piggledy, many of them painted with the names of their former owners. The altar is railed in against the east wall, with pews on either side of it. There are fragmentary remains of seventeenth-century wall paintings. The floor of the church is still laid with fresh straw to keep the building warm.

NY

12. DOLANOG (Ann Griffiths Memorial Chapel), Calvinistic Methodist

Powys (M)

Location: in village on the B4382, 12 miles west of Welshpool and 6 miles south-west of Llanfyllin.
Access: generally open.

The chapel was built in 1903, to a design by G. Dickens-Lewis of Shrewsbury, as a memorial to the well-known writer of hymns. It maintains the traditional liturgical arrangement, with all seating facing the pulpit and communion enclosure, but the detail of the woodwork, the windows and the overall ethos is firmly part of the Arts and Crafts movement of the early twentieth century. A small Sunday schoolroom, again preserving its original furnishings, is separated from the main body of the chapel by folding doors.

NY

13. ELERCH (St Peter), Church in Wales   *Cere.*

Location: on a side road off the A487, 8 miles north-east of Aberystwyth.
Access: key available from the house opposite the church.

The idyllic and remote Leri valley is an unexpected place to find an important Victorian church. It was built by the Revd Lewis Gilbertson, vice-principal of Jesus College, Oxford, who had spent his youth here, and his sisters. As at Llangorwen, he employed William Butterfield as his architect, though here to build a new church, in 1865–8. Although not large, it is tough and ingeniously articulated, with a pyramidal-roofed tower over the choir, around which the complex series of roof shapes is tightly composed. The priest's vestry on the north-east has a circular window, and on the south is a curious tall, narrow transept. It is a pity that the rough local rubble is almost all rendered. The interior is severe, but the excellent east window glass (1868) is by Butterfield's favourite maker, Alexander Gibbs. The reredos is tiled, and the font is of grey marble. Until recently, worship was still ultra-Tractarian, with men and women sitting on opposite sides, and Gregorian chant. The steep-roofed school opposite, with flèche, is by G. E. Street (1856), and the vicarage (1874) is by John Prichard.

PH

14. GLASCWM (St David), Church in Wales   *Powys (R)*

Location: on a side road, 1 mile east of Cregrina (see above).
Access: generally open.

The church, dating largely from the fourteenth and fifteenth centuries and comprising a single-cell nave and chancel with a west tower, is the successor of a former *clas* church. The interior was over-restored in 1891 but still retains a magnificent contemporary roof, ceiled over the eastern bay of the nave and the whole of the chancel. The font is also contemporary with the building and the church has a good ensemble of eighteenth- and nineteenth-century wall tablets by local craftsmen.

NY

15. GUILSFIELD/CEGIDFA (St Aelhaiarn), Church in Wales
Powys (M)

Location: in village on the B4392, 2 miles north of Welshpool.
Access: generally open.

This is one of the largest medieval churches in Mid Wales. The west tower, nave and western portion of the chancel date from c.1300. The south aisle and the two-storey south porch were added in c.1400, and in the late fifteenth century the north aisle was added and the chancel extended eastwards. The chancel and eastern bay of the nave are still covered by a magnificent ceiled roof and much of the timber in the other roofs is also original. The church was very well restored by G. E. Street in 1877–9, largely at the expense of the patrons, Christ Church, Oxford. Street provided the screen, pulpit, low pews, reredos and carved altar table. The altar is raised on steps laid with Minton tiles. The octagonal font is probably thirteenth century. The lean-to hearse house against the south porch dates from 1739.

NY

16. HAFOD (St Michael), Church in Wales   *Cere.*

Location: by itself on the B4574, 2 miles south-east of Devil's Bridge.
Access: generally open.

The church was built in 1803 by Thomas Johnes to serve his family and estate workers. It was burned down in 1932 and rebuilt in 1933 by W. D. Caröe who provided the attractive limed woodwork, comprising the pews, pulpit, north transept screen, lectern, choir stalls, altar rails and sanctuary panelling. Rescued from the first church were the font of 1792, some fragments of sixteenth-century Flemish stained glass from the former east window and part of the monument to Thomas Johnes's daughter by the distinguished sculptor, Sir Francis Chantrey. This had been commissioned in 1812 for £3,150. The house at Hafod was demolished in 1956, but the estate provides a selection of way-marked trails known respectively as the Lady's, Gentleman's and New Walks, laid out between 1789 and 1805.

NY

17. HENFYNYW (St David), Church in Wales   *Cere.*

Location: on the A487, 1 mile south of Aberaeron.
Access: service on Sundays at 10 a.m.

Henfynyw is probably the *Vetus Rubus* which Rhygyfarch, in his *Life of St David* (c.1090), claims to have been the site of St David's education. The name *Hen Fynyw* ('old mynyw' – arguably a Welsh translation of *Vetus Rubus*) implies that the site is in some way a precursor to St David's main monastery of *Menevia* (*Mynyw*). For all its possible historic importance, Henfynyw nowadays is a modest church of simple nave and chancel, rebuilt in 1864–6 by Robert Jewell Withers, replacing an older two-cell structure. The building is of dark stone, dressed with ashlar, standing in a large churchyard, heavily set with modern burials. An ECM (*c.* sixth to ninth century AD) from the site records the name TIGE(I)RN[ACUS].

Inside, the church has a fine chancel arch, gothic timber reredos and an east window by Kempe and Co., *c.*1922. The most striking of the interior fixtures is a font of *c.* twelfth-century, one of a group from Ceredigion, with a square top on an octagonal base and a frieze of rosettes. Outside, the churchyard is entered via a striking lychgate by W. Ellery Anderson (1930). Signboards guide the visitor through the history of the cult of St David in Ceredigion.

JW

18. LAMPETER/LLANBEDR PONT STEFFAN (St Peter), Church in Wales
Cere.

Location: on the north side of the town centre.

Access: services on the first and third Sundays of the month at 8 a.m., 9.30 a.m., 11 a.m. and 5 p.m., and on the second and fourth Sundays at 8 a.m., 10.30 a.m. and 5 p.m.

This grand new church was built, on a fine site above the town, in 1867–9, to replace a 'miserable barn-like structure' of 1836–8 by William Whittington of Neath. The architect was Robert Jewell Withers, a talented London man who built and restored many churches in south and west Wales. It is a tall, strong building – very much a 'town church' – with a commanding south-west tower with pyramidal roof. In Early French Gothic, it is built of rough grey stone, with white dressings. The east window has striking plate tracery. The reredos has mosaics and good furnishings include a stone pulpit. The chancel glass is mostly by Daniel Bell (1870–5). In the south aisle is a window of 1939 by Sir Ninian Comper (St Helena), but the real knockout is the west window glass, dating from 1938–45, which is by the Irish artist Wilhelmina Geddes, a former member of An Túr Gloine. It shows Christ with Saints Peter and

Andrew, and they are very tough and unsentimental, in strong colours. In the porch is a tablet, with piles of books, to the Revd Eliezer Williams, vicar of Lampeter 1805–20, author of several books, who opened a school where he prepared young men for holy orders – a precursor of St David's College.

PH

19. LAMPETER/LLANBEDR PONT STEFFAN (St David's College Chapel), Church in Wales   *Cere.*

Location: in the St David's Building of the University of Wales in the centre of Lampeter.
Access: generally open in term time. Otherwise access may be obtained through the university's main reception desk in the same building.

1. St David's College Chapel, Lampeter. *Chrys Tremthanmor*

The chapel of 1827 by C. R. Cockerell, which forms part of the original college (now university) buildings, was rebuilt by Sir Thomas Jackson in 1880. His are the canopied stalls and the organ screen across the entrance. The east end of the chapel was later refurnished by W. D. Caröe. His war memorial of 1919 and his splendid reredos and altar of 1934 remain *in situ*, though his pulpit of 1922 has recently been removed, as part of a reordering of the sanctuary, and is currently exhibited in the university library. Caröe's reredos replaced a large painting in the style of Correggio, presented to the first chapel in 1827, now hanging in the north aisle added by Jackson.

NY

20. LEIGHTON (Holy Trinity), diocese of Hereford   *Powys (M)*

Location: by itself, off the B4388, 2 miles south-east of Welshpool.
Access: generally open.

The tall broach spire of the church forms a conspicuous landmark on the opposite side of the Severn valley from Welshpool. It was the estate church of Leighton Hall, which was built c.1850–6 by John Naylor, whose wealth came from the Liverpool bank of Leyland and Bullen. He spent enormous sums on the estate, and H. S. Goodhart-Rendel described the church as 'a perfectly preserved and unaltered specimen of nouveau-riche-dom in the 1850s'. The architect of both church and hall was the obscure W. H. Gee of Liverpool. The church, built in 1851–3, is of yellow Cefn stone and is wonderfully elaborate, with flying buttresses, crocketed pinnacles and much rich carving. The lofty interior, beneath its hammerbeam roof, is powerfully atmospheric. The varnished oak pews run right across the nave and narrow triangularly towards the chancel. All doors are covered in red baize. The tiles are by Minton and the colourful stained glass is by Forrest and Bromley of Liverpool. At the south-east corner an octagonal chapel is attached, containing the Naylor monuments. In the centre is a stone angel, carved by Georgina Naylor. The churchyard is surrounded by a ha-ha, and an avenue is aligned onto it from the house, over a mile away.

PH

21. LLANANNO (St Anno), Church in Wales   *Powys (R)*

Location: by itself on the A483, 1 mile north-west of Llanbister (see below).

Access: generally open.

2. Rood loft (*c.*1500), Llananno, St Anno. *Martin Crampin*

The church was completely rebuilt, and largely refurnished, under the direction of David Walker of Liverpool, between 1876 and 1880, but retains one of the finest rood screens and lofts in Wales, dating from c.1500. This was embellished at the restoration by the addition of figures of Christ, his apostles and several Old Testament worthies, and was carefully restored again in 1960. The other pre-Victorian furnishings comprise a fifteenth-century font and a churchwardens' pew of 1681.

NY

22. LLANBADARN FAWR (St Padarn), Church in Wales   *Cere.*

Location: village is by-passed by main Llanbadarn Road; one-way road through village is entered from west end.
Access: generally open.

T hough Llanbadarn Fawr is now absorbed within the inland sprawl of the coastal town of Aberystwyth, it was once the more significant settlement. The imposing cruciform church reflects its status as a former *clas* and the leading intellectual centre of Wales in the eleventh century.

There was probably an early monastery here, dedicated to St Padarn, but Llanbadarn Fawr gained its greatest prominence in the time of Bishop Sulien of St Davids (d.1091), when the *clas* was notable for its scriptorium: producing, amongst other works, the magnificent *Life of St David* (c.1081) by Rhygyfarch ap Sulien, as well as fine manuscripts such as the 'Rhygyfarch Psalter' (now in Dublin). The *clas* gave way to a priory under the governance of St Peter's Gloucester in 1116–17, but the Benedictines were expelled on the death of Henry I in 1135. In 1188 it was described by Gerald of Wales as consisting of secular canons under a lay abbot. In the fourteenth century Llanbadarn Fawr became a possession of Vale Royal Abbey in Cheshire. The church in the fourteenth century features in Dafydd ap Gwilym's poem 'Merched Llanbadarn' ('the girls of Llanbadarn'), in which the poet sees Mass on Sunday as simply an opportunity for ogling.

The present church mostly dates from the thirteenth century, probably after the dissolution of the *clas*, but has the spacious feel of a conventual building. The exterior is strikingly plain, as is the interior of the nave; with simple lancet windows, apart from three Perpendicular windows in the nave, one of which has the rebus of William Stratford, abbot of Vale Royal (1476–1516). The south door, in three orders with keeled shafts, has by far the most notable medieval decoration. The medieval pitch of the roofs was restored by John Pollard Seddon in 1869–84. The pulpit (1879) and the stained glass of the chancel are by Seddon, including the east window (1884) depicting the Transfiguration. The encaustic tiles of the sanctuary make a striking effect in the generally plain interior.

The museum (1989) in the south transept, fronted with glass panels by Peter Lord inscribed with verses from Dafydd ap Gwilym, explains the history of the church and the family of Sulien. It includes two medieval crosses formerly in the churchyard, the decoration of one of which, the Llanbadarn Cross (tenth century) probably reflects the known Irish connections of the *clas* up to the time of Sulien and his family. There is a very large range of seventeenth- and eighteenth-century monuments in the church.

JW

23. LLANBADARN-Y-GARREG (St Padarn), Church in Wales
Powys (R)

Location: by itself on a side road, 2 miles east of Aberedw (see above).
Access: generally open.

A very small, single-cell, late medieval church beside a stream, lightly restored in 1960. The roof and rood beam are original and the latter supports a faded Royal Arms painted on plaster. The simple font is also late medieval, but the pulpit and altar rails date from the seventeenth century.

NY

24. LLANBEDR YSTRAD YW (St Peter), Church in Wales *Powys (B)*

Location: in centre of village, 2 miles north-east of Crickhowell.
Access: generally open.

The church was consecrated in 1060 but was largely rebuilt, and considerably enlarged, in the late fifteenth and early sixteenth centuries. It was rather over-restored by J. L. Pearson in 1897, though he retained the font and south aisle roof of *c*.1500. During the restoration fragments of medieval wall painting over the chancel arch, now exposed, were discovered. The monuments include a delightful eighteenth-century wall tablet recording the death of a child.

NY

25. LLANBISTER (St Cynllo), Church in Wales   *Powys (R)*

Location: in village at junction of A483 and B4356, 6 miles north of
Llandrindod Wells.
Access: generally open.

This large fourteenth-century church is built into the hillside, its west
end raised to compensate for the sloping ground, and with a squat
tower at the east end. It was carefully restored by W. D. Caröe in 1908. He
preserved much of the medieval roof and screen, the eighteenth-century
canopied pulpit and the west gallery of 1716. As well as retaining the
fourteenth-century octagonal font, Caröe added a new, total immersion
baptistery. Beneath the west gallery is a rare survival of a late eighteenth-
or early nineteenth-century schoolroom. The dramatic Christ in Majesty
reredos dates from *c.*1950.

NY

26. LLANDDEWI BREFI (St David), Church in Wales   *Cere.*

Location: in village, on B4343, 7 miles north-east of Lampeter.
Access: open daily, spring–autumn.

One of the most historic churches of Wales, the church of Llanddewi
Brefi is strikingly located on the steep mound that is described in the
Life of St David as where the ground rose under St David's feet at the
legendary Synod of Brefi. Though now the remotest of villages, Llanddewi
Brefi is a natural site for a major church, standing at the end of a natural
route way across the Cambrian mountains and a few miles from a junction
of two Roman roads. The Roman fort of *Bremia* (a Latin form of the name
Brefi) was located nearby.

The range of early monuments around the church allows the visitor to
trace the changes in style and script over the first millennium. The earliest
remains from the church are a Roman monument, cemented into the
bottom of the south wall on the east side of the transept, and an ECM,
cemented into the exterior west wall of the nave at the north corner. The
latter, now broken, is recorded by Edward Lhuyd (1699) as having once
read 'HIC IACET IDNERT FILIVS IACOBI QVI OCCISVS FVIT PROPTER

PREDAM SANCTI DAVVID' ('here lies Idnerth son of James who was killed on account of the plunder of St David'). If correct, this ECM (c. seventh to ninth century) would probably be the earliest reference to St David by name. Later ECMs, probably commemorating important early churchmen, which once stood in the churchyard, are now stored inside the church. One of these records 'CENLISINI BT DS' ('[the Stone of] Cenlisinus May God Bless Him'). This c. ninth-century monument, with its use of mostly rounded letters and Latin contractions, shows the influence of manuscript models over the more angular script of the earlier stones. Later monuments include a modern statue of St David (1959) by Frederick Mancini.

Llanddewi Brefi was a *clas* in the early Middle Ages, refounded as a college of secular canons by Bishop Bek in 1287 which was dissolved at the end of the Middle Ages. The Welsh version of the *Life of David* (*Buchedd Dewi*) was written here in 1346. The tower and crossing with pointed vault, of fourteenth-century date, are remains of the collegiate church of this period. No accompanying range is now visible. The transepts were demolished in the late eighteenth century (north) and 1833 (south); the nave was rebuilt in the latter year, but the whole was remodelled with new roof, windows and porch in 1873–4 by Robert Jewell Withers. The present chancel, with east window in three lights to Saints David, Padarn and Teilo (1962), was built in 1885. The dimensions of the earlier chancel and nave are partly traceable on the exterior of the tower.

JW

27. LLANDEGLEY (Pales Meeting House), Society of Friends Powys (R)

Location: on a side road between the A44 and the A488, 4 miles north-east of Llandrindod Wells.
Access: generally open.

A meeting was established here in 1716 and the present thatched chapel dates from the late eighteenth century. It retains its original benches, tiered at the end of the room, and is one of the most perfectly preserved early Quaker meeting houses in the British Isles. Adjacent to the chapel is a schoolroom of 1867 complete with fireplace.

NY

28. LLANDRINDOD WELLS (Caebach Chapel), Independent

Powys (R)

Location: off North Avenue (A4081) on the northern outskirts of
Llandrindod Wells.
Access: key at neighbouring farmhouse.

The chapel dates from 1715 but the present liturgical arrangement
may not be original. The entrance is in the middle of one of the long
walls and the interior is now arranged with the original pulpit against one
of the short walls in the middle of the communion enclosure. Box pews
are arranged to face the pulpit, and there is tiered seating in a deep gallery
across the opposite short wall.

NY

29. LLANDYFALLE (St Maelog), Church in Wales   *Powys (B)*

Location: on a side road off the A470, 3 miles north-east of Brecon.
Access: generally open.

This fifteenth-century church has an exceptionally broad nave,
retaining its original roof, rood screen and fragments of medieval
stained glass. The altar rails date from the seventeenth century but the
interior is spoilt by very heavy Victorian furnishings and aggressive
tiling. There is a good collection of eighteenth-century wall tablets by
local craftsmen.

NY

30. LLANDYSILIO (St Tysilio), Church in Wales   *Powys (M)*

Location: on the A483, midway between Welshpool and Oswestry.
Access: details of key holder on notice board.

Near the main road from Oswestry to Welshpool stands the new
church designed by G. E. Street to replace the previous one, much
rebuilt in 1833 but already ruinous. Built in 1867–8, of greenish Welshpool

stone with Cefn dressings, it is a superb exercise in refined Decorated Gothic. It consists of nave, chancel and north aisle, with a timber porch; a miniature round tower, with conical roof, stands at the north-west corner. The exterior is carefully and elegantly composed. The rich interior has a tall arcade to the aisle and a cusped arch on the north side of the chancel to the organ chamber. The excellent original fittings include a Caen stone reredos by Thomas Earp, a Bath stone pulpit, altar table and rails, stalls, candelabra, stone cancelli and a wrought-iron lectern. The glass in the east window, made in 1868 by Clayton and Bell, was designed by Street; the west window, by the same makers, is of 1878. On the south side of the nave a window showing Christ walking on the water commemorates four sailors lost in the China Sea while trying to save a shipmate; it is by Powell's, 1879. On the west wall is an exquisite brass plate to Mary Eyton, d.1674, by Silvanus Crue, a Wrexham goldsmith, whose brasses can be seen in several north Wales churches. The epitaph is charming.

PH

31. LLANELIEU (St Ellyw), formerly Church in Wales, now in the care of the Friends of Friendless Churches
Powys (B)

Location: by itself on a side road off the A479, 1 mile east of Talgarth.
Access: key available from the house opposite the church.

This is one of the best preserved medieval churches in Wales, a small single-cell building of the thirteenth century, not restored until 1905 and then very lightly. The church is entered through a magnificent wooden door of c.1600. The nave is separated from the chancel by a fourteenth-century screen, above which is a tympanum painted with a white cross and roses on a red background, and a canopy designed to cover the two side altars that originally stood in front of the screen. The pulpit dates from the seventeenth century, as do the fragmentary wall paintings of the Royal Arms, Ten Commandments and Lord's Prayer.

NY

32. LLANFEUGAN (St Meugan), Church in Wales   *Powys (B)*

Location: by itself on a side road reached from the B4558 in Pencelli,
3 miles south-east of Brecon.
Access: generally open.

The church was built by Ralph de Mortimer in the thirteenth century.
Although much restored by S. W. Williams in 1891, it retains a handsome
fifteenth-century nave roof, the original font and, in the north aisle,
fragments of the former rood screen. The pulpit and choir stalls have been
made up from seventeenth-century woodwork and there is some early
nineteenth-century seating in the north aisle and at the west end of the nave.

NY

33. LLANFIHANGEL-Y-CREUDDYN (St Michael), Church in Wales
Cere.

Location: on a side road between the A4120 and the B4340, 5 miles
south-east of Aberystwyth.
Access: generally open.

A large thirteenth-century cruciform church with a central tower, and
one of the finest surviving medieval buildings in Ceredigion. The
chancel and north transept were rebuilt in *c.*1840, and there were repairs
by R. K. Penson in 1870–4 and further ones by W. D. Caröe in 1932–3. The
chief feature of the interior is the complete set of sixteenth-century roofs.
The heavy, carved reredos dates from 1919.

NY

34. LLANFILO (St Milburga), Church in Wales   *Powys (B)*

Location: on a side road between the A470 and the B4560, 2 miles west
of Talgarth.
Access: generally open.

This attractive fifteenth-century church was carefully restored by
W. D. Caröe and others between 1913 and 1951, and preserves an

exceptional range of high-quality furnishings. There is an original barrel roof in the nave and the sixteenth-century rood screen preserves much of its original coving, though the rood cross and supporting figures were added in 1926–30. A rare survival is the fifteenth-century angelus bell in the chancel. In the nave is a seventeenth-century pulpit and some contemporary benches; also from this date are the altar table and rails, though the table was extended in *c.*1950 to fit the original stone *mensa*. A second *mensa* has been placed on top of the altar in front of the rood screen. The church houses an excellent collection of seventeenth- to nineteenth-century wall tablets.

NY

35. LLANFYLLIN (St Myllin), Church in Wales   *Powys (M)*

Location: in town centre.
Access: generally open.

This is one of the very few eighteenth-century town churches in Wales. It was rebuilt between 1706 and 1714, and is a red-brick structure with stone dressings, lacking a separate chancel. Contemporary with the building is the deep west gallery, its front embellished with boards recording details of the parochial charities. The altar table dates from 1744, but otherwise the church was much, but very interestingly, altered in the nineteenth century. The north transept was added in 1826 to provide accommodation for a girls' school, the boys being taught in the town hall. The major alterations date from 1863–4 when the new transept was made part of the body of the church by the insertion of a two-bay neo-Norman arcade and the sanctuary was separated from the nave by the erection of a three-bay neo-Norman arcade. The altar was provided with neo-Norman rails and a neo-Norman pulpit and reading desk was placed on the south-west side of the new arcade. New seating was provided by open benches, but still arranged in three blocks without a central passageway. This is an exceptionally late date for a town church to be refurnished in such a pre-ecclesiological manner.

NY

36. LLANGASTY TALYLLYN (St Gastayn), Church in Wales *Powys (B)*

Location: on the south shore of Llangors Lake off the A40, 5 miles south-east of Brecon.
Access: generally open.

Situated near the southern end of Llangors Lake (hence Talyllyn), the old church was almost wholly rebuilt in 1848–50, and the school built, at the expense of Robert Raikes of Treberfedd, the house which stands higher up. Raikes was a rich Yorkshireman, who had come under the spell of the Tractarians at Oxford. He bought the estate in 1848 with the intention of introducing their ideas to a part of Wales where churchmanship was at a low ebb. The architect for church, school and house was John Loughborough Pearson, who had built a church in the East Riding for Raikes's grandmother. Family tradition has it that pitch pine was used in the house, instead of oak, so that there would be more money to spend on the church. The small, severe Early English church has a plain west tower, partly ancient. The interior is surprisingly opulent. The stencilled texts on the walls were recently restored. The east window has wall-shafts, and there is a parclose screen of iron. The low chancel screen incorporates bits of the sixteenth-century one. There were daily services, and Welsh ones too on Sundays. Mrs Raikes trained a surpliced choir. The complete fittings by Pearson include even a stoup in the porch.

PH

37. LLANGATWG (St Catwg), Church in Wales *Powys (B)*

Location: in village across the River Usk which now forms a southern suburb of Crickhowell.
Access: generally open.

This large fourteenth- and fifteenth-century double-naved church, with a sturdy west tower and south porch, was well restored in the late nineteenth century and preserves its plastered wagon roofs. Its chief feature is the magnificent collection of eighteenth-century wall tablets, some coloured, and many by members of the Brute family, responsible for many of the wall tablets in the churches of south Breconshire. In the north nave are the remains of the village stocks and whipping post.

NY

38. LLANGORWEN (All Saints), Church in Wales   *Cere.*

Location: in the village of Clarach on the B4572, 2 miles north of Aberystwyth.
Access: services at 11 a.m. on the first, second and fourth Sundays of the month and at 2.30 p.m. on the third.

The land for the church built in 1841 was given by Matthew Davies Williams of Cwmcynfelin, whose brother Isaac, priest and poet, had become a friend of John Keble at Oxford. The new church was designed by Henry Jones Underwood, of Oxford, in the same simple lancet style that he had used for the church he built in 1835–6 for John Henry Newman at Littlemore, where Isaac Williams had been Newman's first curate. At the time of the consecration of Llangorwen it was stated that 'the east window and interior of the chancel is ... formed on the model of the East end of the Church at Littlemore'. Like Littlemore, Llangorwen had a stone altar – the first set up in Wales since the Reformation. The wooden eagle lectern was given by Keble, and the remarkable bronze chandeliers are said to have been given by Newman. The porch and bell turret were added in 1849–50, during the incumbency of Lewis Gilbertson (see Elerch above), and are very characteristic of William Butterfield. The porch has boldly foliated principals in its roof. The glass in the east window, of the 1850s, is probably by Wailes. The intended tower was never built.

PH

39. LLANGURIG (St Curig), Church in Wales   *Powys (M)*

Location: in village on the A44, 4 miles south-west of Llanidloes.
Access: generally open.

This former *clas* church, possibly founded by St Curig in the sixth century, and belonging to the Cistercian abbey of Strata Florida from the late twelfth century, preserves some fifteenth-century features, but was largely rebuilt in 1877–8 under the direction of Sir George Gilbert Scott and Arthur Baker. The roofs of the nave and chancel are adorned with massive angels. The chancel screen was reconstructed from drawings of the former rood screen made by John Parker in 1828, six years before it was dismantled. There is a fine series of ten stained-glass windows, showing scenes from the life of St Curig and incorporating the heraldry of the Lloyd family of Clochfaen, who paid for the restoration of the church, by the leading firm of Burlison and Grylls.

NY

40. LLANIDLOES (St Idloes), Church in Wales   *Powys (M)*

Location: in town centre.
Access: generally open.

The church was almost entirely rebuilt in 1542, when the opportunity was taken to install the thirteenth-century arcade from the dissolved Cistercian church at Abbey Cwmhir between the nave and the north aisle. The nave roof, of the hammerbeam type and incorporating elaborate carved angels, one of the finest in Wales, also dates from 1542, and may also be a reconstruction of a roof formerly at Abbey Cwmhir. The west tower has one of the wooden belfries and pyramidal roofs typical of several Montgomeryshire churches. The church was well restored, under the direction of G. E. Street, in 1880–2 and there is excellent stained glass by the firm of Clayton and Bell in the east window of the chancel.

NY

41. LLANIGON (St Eigen), Church in Wales   *Powys (B)*

Location: in village off the B4350, 2 miles south-west of Hay-on-Wye.
Access: generally open.

The church is entered through a fourteenth-century south porch, to which a bell tower was added in 1670, an exceptionally unusual arrangement. The rest of the church was almost completely rebuilt in

1856–7, in a wholly pre-ecclesiological manner, and preserves its furnishings virtually intact. The pulpit and reading desk, of virtually identical design, the former one step higher than the latter, are placed on opposite sides of the chancel arch. There are low, numbered, box pews in the nave and large family pews in the chancel, although that in the north side has been altered to permit the later installation of an organ and choir stalls. The altar table and rails date from the eighteenth century and there is an early nineteenth-century barrel organ at the west end of the nave. The nave roof is ceiled and there is painted glass of 1856 in the east window of the chancel.

NY

42. LLANSANTFFRAID-YM-MECHAIN (St Brigid), Church in Wales
Powys (M)

Location: in village on the A495, 6 miles east of Llanfyllin.
Access: generally open.

An interesting church, in which the long nave has been extended well to the west of the north aisle and given a wooden belfry. The church was well restored by J. O. Scott, who preserved and restored the barrel roof to the nave and chancel in 1891–3. The seventeenth-century pulpit and tester are handsome examples of their type. The altar rails date from the eighteenth century and the font from the thirteenth century, but most of the other furnishings, including the elaborate chancel screen and loft, date from Scott's restoration.

NY

43. LLANSILIN (St Sulien), Church in Wales
Powys (D)

Location: in village on the B4580, 5 miles west of Oswestry.
Access: generally open.

This handsome late medieval, double-naved church near the English border was carefully restored, under the direction of Arthur Baker, in 1890. He preserved the fifteenth-century roof of the south nave and the elaborate ceiling across the whole of the chancel, and several seventeenth-century furnishings, including the west gallery, the font with its cover and the long altar table, clearly originally placed table-wise with its uncarved end against the east wall of the chancel. Baker also designed the neo-Jacobean pews and choir stalls, reusing much seventeenth-century woodwork in their construction. The former eighteenth-century reredos, incorporating panels inscribed with the Ten Commandments, and pictures of Moses and Aaron, is now in the west gallery. Other interesting furnishings include a painted benefaction board of 1740, the Royal Arms of Queen Anne in plaster, a wooden pillar alms box of 1664 and a two-tier chandelier of 1824.

NY

44. LLANWENOG (St Gwenog), Church in Wales   *Cere.*

Location: off the A475, 6 miles west of Lampeter.
Access: generally open.

3. Medieval font, Llanwenog, St Gwenog. *Martin Crampin*

In a region largely denuded of its medieval fabric by the late nineteenth century, Llanwenog is a fortunate survival. The church lies down a steep slope from the main road, the battlemented tower is all that is

43

visible from a distance – the effect is heightened by the base of the tower being on a higher level than the nave. The curvilinear churchyard is entered by a lychgate of c.1930. The tower, with steep batter, is of late fifteenth-century date. Above the west door is a shield of Rhys ap Thomas (d.1525), who is reputed to have built the tower to commemorate the Battle of Bosworth (1485).

From the rectangular narthex stairs go down to the nave and chancel. The beautiful timber barrel roof is fifteenth century in date; the surviving medieval nave window, with ogee decoration, in the south wall, is c.fourteenth century. Two pointed arches lead to a south-east chapel with two c.fifteenth-century windows in the south wall. In the chapel is a stone font of c.twelfth century with a dramatic frieze of human heads – perhaps the most remarkable of the fine group of Romanesque fonts from Ceredigion. The church has especially fine timber carving. Two early modern panels bear the Commandments and Creed in Welsh in black lettering. The bench ends with various carvings of local symbols and mottoes (1915–19) which were conceived by Mary Davies-Evans of the nearby mansion of Highmead, while the beautiful screen (1915) is by Joseph Reubens, a Belgian refugee at Highmead during the First World War. There is a range of other monuments, many associated with Highmead.

JW

45. LLANWNNOG (St Gwynog), Church in Wales   *Powys (M)*

Location: in village on the B4568, 6 miles west of Newtown.
Access: key available from The Meadows, the bungalow near the church.

Although the church was virtually rebuilt by R. K. Penson in 1863, he preserved one of the finest fifteenth-century rood screens in Wales, complete with its coving, loft and wooden staircase. He also preserved some fragments of medieval stained glass and a cut-down seventeenth-century pulpit, and reused the medieval roof bosses in the ceiled chancel roof. The east window of 1863 is by Evans Brothers of Shrewsbury.

NY

46. MACHYNLLETH (Our Lady Help of Christians), Roman Catholic

Powys (M)

Location: on Newtown Road on edge of town centre.

Access: Mass on Sundays at 11 a.m.

One of the earliest post-Vatican II buildings in Wales, designed by Sir Percy Thomas in 1965. It is a simple rectangular building with a flat roof and ground-to-ceiling windows. The free-standing altar is placed in the middle of the church in front of an internal sacristy and is surrounded by seating, wooden benches on stone supports, on three sides. It is an excellent example of a church that is both devotional and functional at the same time.

NY

47. MAESYRONNEN (Chapel), Independent *Powys (R)*

Location: near Glasbury-on-Wye, on a minor road turning northwards from the A4153 from Glasbury to Llowes, 1 mile east of Glasbury.

Access: generally open.

This is probably the earliest of all Dissenting buildings still in use in Wales, having been built about 1696–7, and possibly rebuilt then from an existing sixteenth-century barn. It was founded with the help of Charles Lloyd, squire of the nearby Maesllwch estate, but its atmosphere is that of yeoman and peasant farmers. Of reddish local stone, it is a single-storey building of five bays, with four mullioned and transomed windows and two doors, above which is a fine stone-tiled roof. Attached to one end is a probably contemporary caretaker's cottage which has a small upper storey. A little chimney divides the slightly higher chapel from the cottage, almost as a nave might be demarcated from a chancel.

Equally remarkable is the chapel interior, which cannot have been much altered from the late seventeenth century, floored with simple stone slabs, a few old box pews here and there, the main seating being open-backed pews (almost like garden seats) and crude benches. The low pulpit is in the centre of one of the long walls, the ancient crucks holding the roof being supported by wooden pillars in the middle of the chapel. On the plain whitewashed walls are a few fine memorial stones. The atmosphere is of a Quakerish simplicity – clean, airy, plain and light.

It sits in its broad grassy graveyard in a remote and beautiful rural setting.

PM

48. MEIFOD (St Mary and St Tysilio), Church in Wales   *Powys (M)*

Location: in village on the A495, 4 miles south of Llanfyllin.
Access: generally open.

The church, consecrated in 1156, was built on the site of a former *clas* church. The eastern part of the nave and the south aisle date from the fourteenth century and preserve their original roofs. The west tower is fifteenth century and the north aisle was rebuilt by Benjamin Ferrey as part of his restoration of the church in 1871–2. The church contains a wealth of interesting furnishings: a ninth-century carved cross slab, possibly reused as the tombstone of Madoc ap Maredudd, prince of Powys, who died in 1160; a fifteenth-century octagonal font; seventeenth-century altar table and rails; a reredos made up from an assemblage of medieval and post-Reformation carved woodwork; an early nineteenth-century 'Gothick' organ case; and panels of heraldic glass, painted by David Evans in 1838, fixed to the aisle windows and showing the coats of arms of the Welsh border families.

NY

49. MONTGOMERY/TREFALDWYN (St Nicholas), Church in Wales
Powys (M)

Location: in town centre.
Access: generally open.

As befits this delightful former county town, with its castle and wealth of Georgian buildings, the church is an ambitious cruciform building of the thirteenth century, with a tower, rebuilt in 1816, placed, unusually, at the north end of the north transept. The nave has retained its sixteenth-century roof, the western part open but the eastern part ceiled. The chancel is separated from the nave by a double screen; the western part, facing the nave, is original to the church and possible contemporary with the nave roof. The eastern part, facing the chancel, complete with its loft, and the choir stalls, all dating from the fifteenth century, come from the former priory church at Chirbury, over the border in Shropshire. The reredos of 1878, with figures by Thomas Earp, incorporates the lower part of the east window of the chancel. The church contains a fine series of fifteenth- and sixteenth-century monuments to members of the Herbert and Mortimer families.

NY

50. MWNT (Holy Cross), Church in Wales *Cere.*

Location: approached by narrow lanes off the A487, 4 miles north of Cardigan.
Access: generally open.

Mwnt's primitive character is evocative of more ancient times. The small church stands in a wild and empty landscape, overlooking steep cliffs and overtopped by a towering, fortified promontory. The building is single cell, entered by a south door with pointed arch; the main fabric *c.*fourteenth century. The six-bay timber truss roof is probably fifteenth century. The church was rebuilt in 1853. Repairs in 1917, following storm damage, uncovered the rood stair in the north wall and a beam from the rood loft with carved heads in niches (fourteenth/fifteenth century). There is a *c.*twelfth-century font of 'table-top' form with scalloped decoration – a type common in Pembrokeshire.

JW

51. OLD RADNOR/PENCRAIG (St Stephen), diocese of Hereford

Powys (R)

Location: by itself on a side road off the A44, 4 miles north-west of Kington (Herefordshire).
Access: generally open.

This is a large and handsome fifteenth-century church comprising a west tower, nave with north and south aisles, a south porch and a chancel with north and south chapels. The roofs of both nave and aisles, complete with carved foliage and emblem bosses, date from the early sixteenth century as does the remarkable organ case, the earliest one surviving in the British Isles. The rood screen and choir stalls date from the late fifteenth century. There are also fragments of medieval stained glass and tiling, and splendid eighteenth-century Italian paintings of Moses and Aaron, probably part of a now dismantled reredos.

NY

52. PARTRISHOW (St Issui), Church in Wales

Powys (B)

Location: at the end of a road, clearly signposted, 3 miles north-east of Llanbedr Ystrad Yw (see above).
Access: generally open.

This is one of the most remarkable churches in Wales and one of the best-preserved medieval ones in the British Isles. It comprises a nave and chancel, with a separate *capel y bedd* at the west end, dating largely from the thirteenth to fifteenth centuries, and carefully restored by W. D. Caröe in 1908–10. The most important features of the church are the roofs and rood screen of *c.*1500. The latter retains not only its loft intact but also the two stone altars standing in front of it, an exceptionally rare survival. Later furnishings include the seventeenth-century pulpit, altar rails and painted texts. The font, which dates from *c.*1055, has an inscription to Cynhillin, lord of Ystrad Yw. The church contains a large number of wall tablets carved by members of the Brute family. The *capel y bedd* retains its original altar built over the shrine of the patron saint.

NY

53. PENBRYN (St Michael), Church in Wales   *Cere.*

Location: by itself on a side road off the A487, midway between
Cardigan and New Quay.
Access: generally open.

A simple thirteenth-century church on the cliffs above the sea, with
whitewashed walls, a medieval nave roof, plastered between the
beams, and a boarded nineteenth-century ceiling over the sanctuary. The
seating is provided by very simple nineteenth-century benches painted
dove grey; the benches themselves were part of a light restoration in
1887–8 by David Davies, their painting that of the further restoration by
A. D. R. Caröe in 1957, which exposed the medieval roof. There are two
square twelfth-century fonts, one originally at Cenarth and later at Sarnau.

NY

54. PENNANT MELANGELL (St Melangell), Church in Wales

Powys (M)

Location: at the end of a side road reached from the B4391 at
Llangynog, 10 miles south-west of Llanfyllin.
Access: generally open.

The twelfth-century church has been much altered over the years and
both its fabric and furnishings now date largely from a vigorous
restoration, practically a rebuilding, in 1877. The pulpit, Royal Arms,
benefactions board and wooden candelabrum date from the eighteenth
century, as do the panels inscribed with the Ten Commandments in
Welsh, now incorporated in the loft of the fifteenth-century rood screen.
The most remarkable feature of the church is, however, the *capel y bedd*
at the east end of the chancel. This contains the twelfth-century shrine of
the patron saint, which was partially reconstructed in 1958–9, and
carefully restored in 1988–92, when the eastern part of the chancel was
reordered to achieve a better relationship between the shrine and the
altar in front of it, and a new eastern apse was built behind the shrine on
the foundations of one that had been demolished.

NY

55. PENRHYNCOCH (St John the Divine), Church in Wales   *Cere.*

Location: in village off the A4159, 4 miles north-east of Aberystwyth.
Access: open occasionally during the summer.

This is a comparatively late work (1880–2) by Robert Jewell Withers, and is a neat little building. Nave and chancel have the same roofline, but the chancel is narrower. The style is Early English. Over the west end is a timber bellcote, supported on a splendid timber frame within the church. There is an alabaster reredos of *c*.1918. There are many tablets to the Pryses of nearby Gogerddan, with the peculiarity that each bears the signature of the person who erected it. The east window, by Hardman, is to Pryse Pryse Pryse (d.1900). The most remarkable of the furnishings is the astonishing lectern, an eagle crushing a dragon, in brightly coloured pottery, on an elaborate stone base. It appears to have been made for Llanbadarn Fawr, at the time of J. P. Seddon's 1880 restoration, perhaps by Doulton's.

PH

56. PENTREBACH (Capel Beilidu), Calvinistic Methodist   *Powys (B)*

Location: by itself on a side road off the A40, 3 miles north of Sennybridge.
Access: the chapel is in the process of being transferred into the custody of the Welsh Religious Buildings Trust from whom further details can be obtained.

This small chapel in the parish of Llandeilo'r Fan was built in 1800 and refitted in 1858. It retains complete furnishings of this date with the pulpit on the long entrance wall, in the middle of the *sêt-fawr*, and tiered box pews arranged to face it. There are no galleries. The adjacent Sunday schoolroom, which preserves its original fireplace and benches, is reached by an external staircase. The chapel is no longer used for worship.

NY

57. PRESTEIGNE/LLANANDRAS (St Andrew), diocese of Hereford

Powys (R)

Location: in town centre.
Access: generally open.

This is one of the finest fifteenth-century town churches in Wales, comprising an aisled nave, south-west tower, chancel and Lady chapel. Between the thirteenth and sixteenth centuries the church belonged to the Augustinian canons of Wigmore Abbey in Herefordshire and this undoubtedly accounts for the richness of its fabric. Part of the east end of the north aisle wall dates from the tenth or eleventh century and is the only surviving remnant of Saxon building work in Wales. The church was restored by J. L. Pearson in 1889–91 and his are the pulpit and screen. A further restoration in 1927 saw the pews replaced by chairs to make the interior more spacious. There are fragments of medieval stained glass and wall paintings and a magnificent early sixteenth-century Flemish tapestry illustrating the triumphant entry of Christ into Jerusalem on Palm Sunday.

NY

58. RHULEN (St David), Church in Wales

Powys (R)

Location: on a side road, 1 mile south of Cregrina (see above).
Access: generally open.

A very simple, almost crude, single-cell church of *c.*1300, externally whitewashed and with leaning walls. The wooden bell turret contains two medieval bells. The altar is formed by a stone recess in the windowless east wall. The roof is ceiled and there is an octagonal font of *c.*1400.

NY

59. SOAR-Y-MYNYDD (Chapel), Calvinistic Methodist   *Cere.*

Location: signed from the mountain road between Llanwrtyd Wells and Tregaron, 8 miles south-east of the latter.
Access: generally open.

4. Chapel, Soar-y-Mynydd. *Jonathan Wooding*

This remote mountain chapel of 1822–8, on the border of the parishes of Llanddewibrefi and Tregaron, retains its original box pews, *sêt-fawr* and plastered ceiling, in an ungalleried interior. The late nineteenth-century low balustraded pulpit is in the middle of the long entrance wall with a painted inscription, 'God is love' in Welsh (*Dyw cariad yw*), painted on the wall behind it.

NY

60. TRELYSTAN (St Mary), diocese of Hereford *Powys (M)*

Location: by itself on a side road off the B4388, 2 miles south-east of Leighton (see above).
Access: generally open.

This fifteenth-century timber-framed church, situated very near the English border, is unique in Wales. Though heavily restored in 1856, it retains its original roof and part of a fifteenth-century screen formerly in the chancel at Chirbury, as well as seventeenth-century three-sided altar rails and a delightful miniature barrel organ of 1827. The east window contains fine, Munich-style stained glass, possibly by David Evans, showing the Agony in the Garden.

NY

2

Churches and Chapels in North-East Wales

61. BETTISFIELD (St John the Baptist), Church in Wales   *Flint.*

Location: on a side road between the A495 and the B5063, 4 miles east of Ellesmere.
Access: open April to September, 8.30 a.m. to 7 p.m.; October to March, 8.30 a.m. to 4 p.m.

This church was built in 1872–4 by Lord and Lady Hanmer of Bettisfield Park. Their architect was G. E. Street, and the result is a fine example of his mature work, in Early Decorated Gothic style. It is not large, but the square tower, with its elegant octagonal spire, and the skilful massing give it great character. Inside, the north chapel and tower on the other side are treated as transepts to the nave, which provides spatial interest. Original furnishings include the Caen stone reredos, with beautiful Minton tiles on either side, and the stained glass of east and west windows, by Clayton and Bell. Only the transept screen is later. The lychgate, in timber and tiles, is also by Street.

PH

62. BODELWYDDAN (St Margaret), Church in Wales   *Flint.*

Location: on the north side of the A55, 2 miles north-west of St Asaph.
Access: generally open.

The gleaming white limestone spire (202 feet high) is a notable landmark on the north Wales coast. What Edward Hubbard called 'the ultimate in splendiferous estate churches' was built in 1856–60 by Margaret, Lady Willoughby de Broke, at a cost of almost £30,000, in memory of her husband. She was the daughter of Sir John Williams of Bodelwyddan Castle. Her architect was John Gibson (best known for his banks), who had worked for the Willoughby de Brokes at Compton Verney. The spire is based on King's Sutton, Northamptonshire, and the church, in correct Decorated Gothic, has little to do with Wales. Inside, there is much marble, including the Belgian red arcade piers, and elaborate carving of stone and wood. Pulpit and stall ends are by Thomas Earp. The extraordinary eagle lectern is by T. H. Kendall of Warwick (1882). The white marble font, of 1862, by Peter Hollins, represents the two daughters of Sir Hugh Williams, holding a shell. There is good glass (including the east window) by M. and A. O'Connor, and less good by Ward and Hughes. The south chapel was furnished as a war memorial by W. D. Caröe (1924). Beneath the tower is a bust of Lady Willoughby de Broke by Matthew Noble (1855). In the churchyard are the graves of eighty-three Canadian soldiers: most died of the flu, but five were killed in rioting caused by delays in returning home. The vicarage and school are probably also by Gibson.

PH

63. BUCKLEY/BWCLE (St Matthew), Church in Wales   *Flint.*

Location: in town centre.
Access: services on Sundays at 8 a.m. and 10.30 a.m.

This is an excellent example of John Douglas's genius for transforming an unpromising structure into a church of real character. In 1821–2 the Church Commissioners paid for a church of nave, chancel and tower by John Oates (of Halifax). As the industries of Buckley flourished, this was altered in 1845 by James Harrison, and again in 1874–5. After Canon Drew, son-in-law of W. E. Gladstone, became vicar, the church was completely remodelled by Douglas and Minshull. In 1900–1 an apsidal chancel was built, in memory of Gladstone. In 1902 the tower was altered and a porch was built with the proceeds of the publication of John Ruskin's letters to Mrs Drew. Then, in 1904–5, the nave was given arcades of steel columns clad in timber, supporting a timber clerestory (probably for lightness).

The light and spacious interior has charming painted decoration below the clerestory and in the baptistery (the latter designed by Douglas and executed by W. F. Lodge). There is excellent stained glass by Henry Holiday in the apse (1899–1901), baptistery (1901–2) and the west window of the north aisle (1909–10). The stalls and pulpit are typical of Douglas, but the reredos and other sanctuary fittings have an Art Nouveau flavour. The timber lychgate dates from 1902. The clock was designed (like the Big Ben clock) by Lord Grimthorpe.

PH

64. CAERWYS (St Michael), Church in Wales *Flint.*

Location: in village on the B5122, 8 miles north-east of Denbigh.
Access: generally open.

This largely fourteenth-century church comprises nave, chancel, north aisle and north-west tower. Though over-restored in 1894–5, it retains a font of 1661, altar table of 1620 and seventeenth-century woodwork incorporated in the pulpit, cancelli and sanctuary panelling. There are also remains of three fourteenth-century sepulchral slabs and fragments of medieval stained glass in the easternmost south window of the chancel.

NY

65. CILCAIN (St Mary), Church in Wales *Flint.*

Location: in village on a side road between the A494 and A541, 4 miles west of Mold.
Access: generally open.

This late medieval double-naved church, with a north-west tower, was well restored by John Douglas in 1888–9. His are the screens between the north and south naves, the neo-Jacobean pews, the simple pulpit and the choir stalls incorporating panels of seventeenth-century carved woodwork. The chief feature of the church, however, is the magnificent fifteenth-century hammerbeam roof across the south nave, supported by carved angels and other figures, the section over the chancel being wagon-ceiled. There are also stained-glass representations of the Crucifixion, Our Lady, St John, St Peter and St George, dated 1546, in the east window of the chancel. Either side of this window are handsome eighteenth- and nineteenth-century wall tablets to members of the Mostyn family. Unusual survivals are boards of 1809 inscribed with the Ten Commandments in English, and the Creed, Lord's Prayer and scripture texts in Welsh.

NY

5. Carved ceiling (fifteenth century), Cilcain, St Mary. *Martin Crampin*

66. DENBIGH/DINBYCH (St Marcella), Church in Wales   *Denb.*

Location: on western outskirts of Denbigh reached from the town by-pass (A525).
Access: generally open.

An exceptionally handsome late medieval double-naved church with a west tower and its original roofs, that of the south nave having an elaborate cornice. The font and the elaborate altar table, railed on three sides, at the east end of the south nave, dated from the seventeenth century. The church was well restored in 1908 by C. Hodgson Fowler, who incorporated parts of the former medieval rood screen into new screens across both naves, and separating the north and south chancels. The tall canopied pulpit dates from 1683 but looks later. There is also a seventeenth-century parish chest and very elaborate benefaction boards of 1720, similar to that at Gresford (see below). There are fragments of medieval glass in the east window of the north chancel. The church has a splendid collection of monuments, including the brass of Richard Myddleton, governor of Denbigh Castle, who died in 1575, the table tomb of Sir John Salusbury, who died in 1578, and wall tablets to the antiquary Humphrey Llwyd (d.1568) and Robert Salusbury (d.1802). There are also several surviving hatchments to members of the Myddleton and Salusbury families.

NY

67. DERWEN (St Mary), formerly Church in Wales, now in care of Friends of Friendless Churches *Denb.*

Location: in village on a side road between the A494 and the B5105, 6 miles south-west of Ruthin.
Access: generally open.

This broad single-cell fifteenth-century church preserves one of the finest late medieval rood screens and lofts in Wales, in which the socket for the rood crucifix itself, removed after the Reformation, survives. The font and cover date from 1665. In the churchyard are a fifteenth-century schoolroom and a contemporary high cross with carved scenes of the Crucifixion, Baptism of Christ, Coronation of the Blessed Virgin Mary in heaven, and St Michael weighing souls incorporated into it.

NY

68. GRESFORD (All Saints), Church in Wales *Wrex.*

Location: in village off the A483, 2 miles north of Wrexham.
Access: generally open.

This is one of the most handsome fifteenth-century churches in Wales, completed in *c.*1500 and comparable in style with many of the larger churches in neighbouring Cheshire, and which houses a particularly important collection of furnishings. The excellent late medieval roofs were restored by F. H. Crossley in 1929–31. Contemporary with the roofs are the font, rood screen and loft, parclose screen and choir stalls, complete with their misericords. The stone pulpit was designed by G. E. Street as part of his model restoration of the church in 1865–7. The slightly later reredos was designed in 1879 by John Douglas. The north chapel furnishings of 1913–14 are by W. D. Caröe. The chandeliers in the nave date from 1747 and 1796, and the chancel corona and standard candlesticks from 1892. Particularly interesting is the delightful painted board of 1731 recording gifts of plate and furnishings to the church, as well as charitable and educational bequests to the parish. The windows contain an interesting and important mix of medieval and Victorian stained glass, though sadly much of the former was badly damaged in 1966 when the windows were cleaned using an inappropriate detergent. The most important of the medieval glass is in the east windows of the chancel and the north and south aisles. The Victorian glass includes work by Clayton and Bell, C. E. Kempe and Heaton, Butler and Bayne. The large range of monuments includes some unusual wooden ones.

NY

69. HALKYN (St Mary), Church in Wales   *Flint.*

Location: on the south side of the A55, midway between Holywell and Mold.

Access: service on Sundays at 11.15 a.m.

The Halkyn estate belonged to the Grosvenors of Eaton Hall, who built the castle to live in while attending Holywell races. The church was commissioned from John Douglas by his chief patron, the first duke of Westminster. Built in 1877–8, at the huge cost of £23,000, it is impressively sited on the hillside. The stout tower, with its pyramidal roof, is unusually sited at the north-east corner. The church is in the style of c.1300 and beautifully detailed. The south side of the chancel has a continuous arcade of six windows. The interior is lined with the same yellow sandstone as the exterior. The nave is broad, with a fine arched-braced roof. The furnishings are characteristic of Douglas, combining elements from late Gothic, seventeenth-century furniture and the late Victorian aesthetic movement. The stained glass is by Heaton, Butler and Bayne, and all except the east window is delicately painted in monochrome. The former rectory (1885) is by Douglas's pupil E. A. Ould.

PH

70. HAWARDEN/PENARLÂG (St Deiniol), Church in Wales   *Flint.*

Location: in village on the A550, 6 miles north-east of Mold.
Access: generally open.

This fifteenth-century cruciform church, with its central tower and aisled nave, is the finest example of a Tractarian restoration of a medieval church in Wales. The impetus for this came from the local landowner, antiquary and ecclesiologist, Sir Stephen Glynne, whose notes of the many churches he visited over a period of nearly fifty years are preserved in the adjacent St Deiniol's Library. The restoration was begun under the direction of James Harrison in 1855–6, but was continued after a fire in 1857 by Sir George Gilbert Scott, the completed church being reopened in 1859. The choir stalls are by Harrison and are excellent copies of fifteenth-century work, the clergy stall incorporating an elaborate sixteenth-century bench-end. The other furnishings are mostly by Scott and include his slightly later reredos of 1873. In 1915–16 Scott's grandson, Sir Giles Gilbert Scott, designed the rood beam with its figures and candlesticks. The handsome neo-classical pulpit of 1951 was designed by H. S. Goodhart-Rendel. The windows include much Victorian glass of high quality, including the magnificent west window, designed by Burne-Jones in 1898 in memory of Sir Stephen Glynne's brother-in-law and former Liberal prime minister, W. E. Gladstone. In 1901–6 an octagonal chapel was erected at the east end of the north aisle to contain the magnificent monument to Gladstone and his wife. Incorporated in the easternmost wall of this chapel is a stone altar, specifically designed so that the chapel would emulate a late medieval chantry chapel.

NY

71. HOLT (St Chad), Church in Wales   *Wrex.*

Location: in village off the A534, 4 miles north-east of Wrexham.
Access: generally open.

An exceptionally handsome late fifteenth-century church with no break between the aisled nave and chancel, the aisles extending the whole length of the church. Apart from the late medieval roof to both nave and chancel, the contemporary chest with four locks and the fine fifteenth-century font with heraldic carvings, the other furnishings date from the church's competent restoration by Ewan Christian and John Douglas in 1871–3.

NY

72. LLANARMON-YN-IÂL (St Germain), Church in Wales   *Denb.*

Location: in village on the B5431, 4 miles south-east of Ruthin.
Access: generally open.

The late medieval church was rebuilt on the original plan in 1733–40. It retains its original classical windows on the north and south walls, the wooden arcade between the two naves supporting medieval roofs, a marble baluster font and a handsome Royal Arms. There are two large medieval chests and an exceptionally rare and delicate pre-Reformation chandelier incorporating a canopied figure of the Blessed Virgin Mary. The splendid array of monuments includes an early fourteenth-century effigy of Gruffydd ap Llywelyn ab Ynyr of Bodidris and an early seventeenth-century wall tablet with a recumbent effigy and Welsh inscription to Evan Llwyd of Bodidris.

NY

73. LLANBEDR DYFFRYN CLWYD (St Peter), Church in Wales

Denb.

Location: on the A494, 2 miles east of Ruthin.

Access: generally open.

The traveller coming down the Clwydian Hills on the way from Mold to Ruthin rounds a steep bend, to be confronted by a wondrously spiky little church of the most enthusiastic High Victorian character. Built of chunky grey limestone, with bands of polychromatic stone, and striped slate roofs, it has an apse and, on the road side, a low tower surmounted by a hexagonal spirelet with sprouting crockets. The church was built in 1863 for John Jesse of Llanbedr Hall; his architects were the partners John Wilkes Poundley, county surveyor of Montgomeryshire, and David Walker of Birkenhead. The interior does not match the exterior for excitement, but there are tiles by Maw and some first-rate glass, including the chancel windows by Clayton and Bell, and two windows on the south side of the nave by Shrigley and Hunt (the one-light window designed by Carl Almquist, 1887). The tablet to Edward Lloyd, with portrait relief, is signed 'Gwaith J. Gibson, R.A., Rhufain, 1863'. Gibson, born in Conwy, worked in Rome.

PH

8. Llanbedr Dyffryn Clwyd, St Peter. *Martin Crampin*

74. LLANDYRNOG (St Tyrnog), Church in Wales   *Denb.*

Location: in village on the B5429, 4 miles south-east of Denbigh.
Access: generally open.

The Perpendicular double-naved church is typical of the area, but of particular interest because of its restoration in 1876–8 by William Eden Nesfield. His name was presumably suggested by H. R. Hughes, one of the chief funders, for whom Nesfield had built Kinmel Park. He clad the church in pink pebbledash, and provided a new bellcote and west window. The timber-framed porch (reusing two old roof trusses) is decorated with his characteristic sunflowers and what he called 'pies' (roundels derived from Japanese sources). He rebuilt the arcade inside, and provided the font, pulpit, lectern and stalls. The latter have more sunflowers, and a wonderful bench in the chancel has pies. There are rich tiles both on the floor and on the walls flanking the altar. The doors have good ironwork. The stained glass of *c.*1500 in the east window of the north nave was restored and rearranged by C. E. Kempe. The Annunciation in the tracery is particularly fine.

PH

75. LLANELIDAN (St Elidan), Church in Wales   *Denb.*

Location: in village on the B5429, 6 miles south of Ruthin.
Access: generally open.

An unusual fifteenth-century double-naved church, its north nave extending further to the west than the south nave; this extension has been turned into a vestry and supports a double bellcote. The arcade and roofs are original, the latter incorporating an elaborate ceilure over the east end of the north nave. Parts of the former rood screen have been incorporated into the screen between the north nave and the vestry. The font is contemporary with the building and the pulpit and altar rails date from the seventeenth century. The church remained unrestored until 1938 when G. R. Griffith removed most of the box pews, retaining some and reordering them in the south nave, and incorporating other old woodwork into the reredos. There are fragments of medieval stained glass in the east windows of both naves and in the window of the vestry screen. Large boards are inscribed with the Ten Commandments, Creed and Lord's Prayer in Welsh.

NY

76. LLANFAIR DYFFRYN CLWYD (St Cynfarch and St Mary), Church in Wales *Denb.*

Location: in village on the A525, 2 miles south of Ruthin.
Access: generally open.

The double-naved Perpendicular church has a stout tower of the early sixteenth century. One window on the south side is dated 1616. The church is given special interest by its sensitive restoration in 1870–2 by John Dando Sedding, a pupil of Street and one of the best late nineteenth-century church architects. He added the timber south porch and reconstructed the roofs, reusing old timbers. His new furnishings are Perpendicular in style and of good, simple character. The alabaster reredos has unfortunately been painted. The tiles in the sanctuary are by Godwin of Lugwardine. The medieval rood screen partially survives (in the south nave). One window has fragments of glass dating from 1503, while the east window of the north nave is by N. H. J. Westlake, but the treasure of the church is the marvellous window in the south nave by Christopher Whall, the outstanding Arts and Crafts stained-glass artist. It shows Christ blessing the children (1893). An early fourteenth-century tomb slab commemorates Dafydd ap Madog, and there is a curious Grecian tablet to John Hughes (d.1830) by John Gibson's brother Solomon. The lychgate dates from 1708, and the vestry house from 1831.

PH

77. LLANGAR (All Saints), formerly Church in Wales, now in the custody of Cadw *Denb.*

Location: by itself in a field off the B4401, 2 miles south-west of Corwen.
Access: by arrangement from the chapel at Rûg (see below).

This small pre-Reformation church was largely rebuilt and completely refurnished in the late seventeenth and early eighteenth centuries. The furnishings have been preserved largely intact and include box pews, a three-decker pulpit in the middle of the south wall, altar table and rails, and a west gallery for the musicians and singers. The eighteenth-century plaster has been removed to expose a fine medieval roof. The wall paintings have been conserved and rearranged so as to reveal both the pre-Reformation paintings and the post-Reformations texts that previously covered them.

NY

78. LLANGWYFAN (St Cwyfan), Church in Wales   *Denb.*

Location: by itself off the B5429, 4 miles east of Denbigh.
Access: open from Easter to the end of October.

This small pre-Reformation church was conservatively refitted in 1859 with low box pews, a pulpit on the north and a reading desk on the south side of the nave, seats for singers at the west end, a cupboard altar and metal candle sconces on the walls. The south porch is dated 1714. An interesting feature is the eighteenth-century font, almost certainly of foreign manufacture, decorated with biblical scenes.

NY

79. LLANGYNHAFAL (St Gynhafal), Church in Wales   *Denb.*

Location: adjacent to a farm off the B5429, 4 miles north-east of Ruthin.
Access: generally open.

Although unpleasantly rendered externally, this fifteenth-century double-naved church has a much more interesting interior. The original roof, supported by carved angels, and font survive, and there are some good seventeenth-century furnishings, including the pulpit and an unusual railed box pew at the west end of the north nave. The church was well restored by Arthur Baker in 1884. The reredos of 1902 incorporates some seventeenth-century panels and an elaborate pelican in its piety over the central panel. The handsome parish chest dates from the fourteenth century.

NY

80. LLANRHAEADR-YNG-NGHINMEIRCH (St Dyfnog), Church in Wales
Denb.

Location: in village off the A525, 3 miles south-east of Denbigh.
Access: generally open.

A very short sixteenth-century double-naved church with a short north-west tower. It has excellent contemporary roofs, with a ceilure over the east end of the south nave, a timber north porch and a complete Jesse window at the east end of the north nave. The church was well restored by Arthur Baker in 1879–80 when it was fitted with neo-Jacobean furniture. The carved pelican of 1762 was formerly suspended over the altar. There is a late medieval parish chest with an attached poor box. The seventeenth-century font is still largely medieval in style. There is a handsome classical monument to Maurice Jones, who died in 1702.

NY

81. LLANYNYS (St Saeran), Church in Wales
Denb.

Location: by itself on a side road between the A525 and the B5429, 4 miles north of Ruthin.
Access: generally open.

A late medieval double-naved church, the arcade of which was replaced by a series of wooden columns in 1768. The font and roofs are original. There are two seventeenth-century altar tables, one in the north and one in the south naves, and much seventeenth-century woodwork reused in the choir stalls. There is also a late seventeenth-century pulpit and two wooden chandeliers, one with a painted inscription of 1749. The church also retains a Royal Arms of Charles II, a fourteenth-century sepulchral slab, a parish chest of 1687, eighteenth-century charity boards in English and Welsh and a rare pair of eighteenth- or early nineteenth-century dog tongs, used for removing dogs from church services. A fifteenth-century painting of St Christopher was formerly covered by a seventeenth-century Welsh text panel, but this has now been removed and separately conserved.

NY

82. PANTASAPH (St David), Roman Catholic   *Flint.*

Location: off the A55, 2 miles south-west of Holywell.
Access: generally open.

In 1846 Viscount Fielding (later eighth earl of Denbigh) married Louise Pennant, heiress of Downing (Thomas Pennant's house). They decided to build a church and rectory at Pantasaph and work began in 1849, to the design of T. H. Wyatt. Archdeacon Manning preached at the laying of the foundation stone. However, in the next year the Fieldings converted to Rome, and gave the church to the Catholics. The Church of England lost the resulting lawsuit, but enough subscriptions came in to build two substitute churches, also by Wyatt (Brynford and Gorsedd). The Pantasaph church, opened in 1852, is much more vigorous than Wyatt's usual rather bland style. It has a good pyramidal spire, of stone, in the corner between aisle and chancel. To provide a proper Catholic interior, A. W. N. Pugin was called in, and designed high altar, font, pulpit, Lady chapel altar and statues, made by George Myers, and all shown in the Medieval Court of the Great Exhibition, and also a rood screen. Pulpit and screen have gone, and the high altar was replaced in 1893 by one designed by A. E. Purdie, as a memorial to Lord Denbigh, who is commemorated by a monument with effigy, also designed by Purdie, and carved by Boulton and Sons. The Hardman glass in the east window dates from 1852; they replaced the aisle windows in 1882. There is also a window by Harry Clarke of Dublin (1931), and one by his studio (1934). The church was entrusted to the Capuchin Franciscans, whose friary was built in 1858–65, to the design of Benjamin Bucknall. On the hill are Stations of the Cross (1875).

PH

83. PENTROBIN/PENYMYNYDD (St John the Evangelist), Church in Wales   *Flint.*

Location: by itself on the A550, 3 miles south of Hawarden.
Access: details advertised on church notice board.

This idiosyncratic church was built in 1843 at the expense of Sir Stephen Glynne, of Hawarden Castle, well known as an ecclesiastical antiquary.

His architect was John Buckler, best known as an antiquarian artist. Despite their expertise, the result is rather thin, Early English in style, with a spindly spire at the west end. More lavish touches include the octagonal stone-vaulted vestry, the west gallery on stone arcading, the stone altar and the rich sedilia. The church is particularly notable for the interior decoration, carried out by the curate-in-charge, Revd J. E. Troughton, who was here from 1843 until 1864. A tablet was erected by W. E. Gladstone (who had taken over Hawarden Castle from his brother-in-law Glynne because of his financial problems): it records that Troughton 'used his rare gifts of genius and taste in himself adorning all the interior . . . by colouring and frescoes and sculptures and window staining, with much labour but with no detriment to the faithful discharge of his manifold parish duties'. The decorative scheme was designed by Richard Popplewell Pullan, brother-in-law of William Burges. Some of the paintings are copied from the Nazarene Friedrich Overbeck. Troughton made the screen and all the glass except the east and west windows. The painted decoration has suffered from incompetent 'restoration'. The vicarage, of 1846, and school, of 1844 (altered), are presumably also by Buckler.

PH

84. RHYDYMWYN (St John the Evangelist), Church in Wales   *Flint.*

Location: on the A541, 3 miles north-west of Mold.
Access: services on the first and second Sundays of the month at 9.30 a.m., on the third at 8 a.m. and on the fourth at 11 a.m.

This village on the road from Mold to Denbigh has a distinguished example of the High Victorian phase of the work of John Loughborough Pearson. The site was given by Philip Davies-Cooke of Gwysaney, who married in 1862 the daughter of Sir Tatton Sykes, who had employed Pearson to restore churches on his Yorkshire estates. The church was built in 1860–3. In contrasting grey and yellow stone, it consists of nave and chancel, with tall west bellcote. In character it is very French, with plate tracery. Despite its small size, the church has great dignity and presence. The chancel is lined inside with ashlar, with banding in dark stone. The characteristic fittings include the reredos, incised in red and white to represent the Last Supper, the Caen stone and marble pulpit, and the carved stone font. Although Pearson made designs for the vicarage and school, they were built by T. H. Wyatt.

PH

85. RHYL (St Thomas), Church in Wales   *Denb.*

Location: in Russell Road, Rhyl.
Access: generally open.

The small Holy Trinity Church, built in 1835 by Thomas Jones (of Chester), with its cast-iron traceried windows, had 'transept' extensions added in 1850 and 1852, giving it a curious cruciform plan, but the resort was growing so fast that it was still too small, and so the grand and lofty church of St Thomas was built in 1861–9, to the design of George Gilbert Scott. In place of the intended stone spire, Scott added in 1874 the striking shingled, square clock-stage and broach spire (203 feet high), which forms a bold landmark on the flat shore. The spacious interior is in Scott's severe lancet and plate tracery style, with a clerestory of foiled circles, and arcades with aisled shafts and well-carved foliage capitals. Original fittings include the carved alabaster reredos, the stalls, the gorgeous alabaster and marble pulpit and the marble font. The stained glass is mostly by Ward and Hughes. The south-east chapel was fitted up, and vestries were added, in 1910 by John Oldrid Scott.

PH

86. RÛG (Holy Trinity), private chapel now in the custody of Cadw
Denb.

Location: by itself off the A494, 2 miles north-west of Corwen.
Access: April–September, Wednesdays–Sundays and Bank Holiday Mondays, 10 a.m.–5 p.m.

This very important chapel was built by the Salusbury family in 1637 and restored in 1855. It preserves its magnificent seventeenth-century roofs, supported by carved angels, its benches, canopied pews either side of the altar and its west gallery for musicians and singers. The nineteenth-century additions include the stained glass, the screen between the nave and chancel and the pulpit-lectern which it incorporates.

NY

87. RUTHIN/RHUTHUN (St Peter), Church in Wales   *Denb.*

Location: in town centre.
Access: generally open.

Though heavily restored by R. K. Penson in 1854–9 the church retains its fourteenth-century arcade between the nave and north aisle and the magnificent sixteenth-century roofs over both. There is also a handsome altar table of 1621 and several good seventeenth- to nineteenth-century monuments to members of local families. The furnishings provided by Penson include an extremely ornate font. There is also much stained glass of the 1850s by William Wailes and James Powell.

NY

88. RUTHIN/RHUTHUN (Pendref Chapel), Independent   *Denb.*

Location: in town centre.
Access: services on every Sunday except the fourth in the month at 10 a.m. and on the second and fourth Sundays at 2.30 p.m.

A handsome chapel, built in 1827 and renovated in 1875. The bow-fronted entrance wall has a central portico. The late Victorian interior has a large pulpit and *sêt-fawr*, a U-shaped gallery, open benches and a delightful painted ceiling. In the classical niche behind the minister's seat is the inscription: '*Yr Arglwydd yw fy Mugail*' ('The Lord is my Shepherd')

NY

89. ST ASAPH/LLANELWY (St Asaph Cathedral), Church in Wales

Denb.

Location: in town centre.
Access: open daily, 9 a.m.–6 p.m.

The late medieval cruciform cathedral, one of the smallest in Britain, was largely rebuilt during Sir George Gilbert Scott's vigorous restoration in 1869–75, though he retained, much repaired, the fifteenth-century choir stalls. There is also a handsome eighteenth-century iron chest and a large collection of monuments. Scott's interior was cluttered and over-pewed. In recent years the interior has been made much more spacious by the removal of the nave pews and their replacement by chairs. Scott's furnishings include the canopied bishop's throne, pulpit, eagle lectern and high-altar reredos, incorporating an alabaster relief of the procession to Calvary by Thomas Earp. The organ case, which takes up most of the space in the north transept, dates from 1966. Although the cathedral lacks grandeur it is a pleasant building providing an excellent setting for Anglican worship.

NY

90. SHOTTON (St Ethelwold), Church in Wales

Flint.

Location: in a suburb of Queensferry.
Access: open on Thursdays, 10 a.m.–12 noon.

This industrialised area is a surprising place to find one of the best churches by Douglas and Minshull. The project was initiated by W. E. Gladstone (of the nearby Hawarden Castle), but he died before it was built in 1898–1902. The style is Early English, often chosen by Douglas in preference to his more usual late Gothic, and treated in his individualistic way. It is of red sandstone, inside and out. The church is a striking example of his trick of making the chancel (here with a canted apse) higher than the nave, and the roof of the north-east chapel is higher than the north aisle. A picturesque tower and spire were proposed beside the chancel, but only the lower part was built in 1924. The nave has a clerestory, and the mouldings of the arcade die into the piers. Good furnishings include the stone pulpit and font, the painted wooden reredos and carved wooden stalls (1908). The stained glass at the west end, below the gallery, is by Edward Frampton, but it is not known who did the apse glass. The Crucifixion window was given by the Byron Society to commemorate the freedom of Crete. The nearby school was built by Douglas in 1875 (later enlarged).

PH

91. TREFNANT (Holy Trinity), Church in Wales　　　　　*Denb.*

Location: in village on the A525, 3 miles south of St Asaph.
Access: generally open.

This richly decorated church was built in 1853–5 in memory of Colonel and Mrs Salisbury of Galltfaenan Hall, by their daughters. Their architect was George Gilbert Scott. Although there is no tower, character is given to the exterior by the bellcote over the chancel arch and the gables over the aisle windows. The nave has Anglesey marble columns with splendid capitals. These were carved by J. Blinstone of Denbigh who, after studying thirteenth-century French carving at the Architectural Museum in London, under Scott's direction, came back and 'applied the same principles to his own work, arranging every group of leaves from natural specimens, gathered as they were needed from the woods and hedges around'. This was a very early example of Ruskin's influence. The marble pulpit and font are typical of Scott. The east windows of chancel and south aisle have glass by Wailes. Others have grisaille glass by Powell's, and there are three windows by Burlison and Grylls (1885). The chancel was refitted in the early twentieth century: it was 'decorated' in 1901, the choir stalls are of 1909 and the panelling of 1931. It has a marble floor. How much of this is by Sir Giles Gilbert Scott, who added the vestry in 1905 and designed the war memorial tablet and north aisle screen in 1921, is not clear. The rectory and school (1860) are also by Scott, forming a characteristic parochial group.

PH

92. TREMEIRCHION (Corpus Christi), Church in Wales   *Denb.*

Location: in village on the B5429, 3 miles south-east of St Asaph.
Access: generally open.

A long north transept was added to this small single-cell fourteenth-century church in 1864. The medieval furnishings include the font, the arch-braced roof over the nave and chancel and two handsome monuments, one a late thirteenth-century effigy of a knight, probably Sir Robert Pounderling, and the other a late fourteenth-century canopied tomb and effigy of a priest, Dafydd ap Hywel ap Madog, in full eucharistic vestments. Salusbury hatchments hang either side of the organ on the west wall of the nave. There are fragments and panels of fifteenth- and seventeenth-century stained glass in two windows. In the churchyard is a splendid fourteenth-century cross on a new base, with the Crucifixion, Our Lady and St John on one side, Our Lady of Walsingham on the other and figures of bishops between them. The original cross base was converted to serve as a sundial in 1748.

NY

93. WORTHENBURY (St Deiniol), Church in Wales   *Wrex.*

Location: by itself on the B5069, 6 miles south-east of Wrexham.
Access: generally open.

T he church was rebuilt in 1736–9 with a broad nave, shallow eastern apse and a west tower. Apart from the west gallery, erected in 1830, all the furnishings are contemporary with the building and it is one of the finest pre-Victorian church interiors in Wales. On either side of the nave are double blocks of box pews, with a three-decker pulpit on the south side. There are family pews at the east end of the nave and, complete with fireplaces, in the chancel. The handsome plaster ceiling incorporates a dove in a glory in the apse, and there is a mixture of heraldic and salvaged medieval glass in the east window.

NY

94. WREXHAM/WRECSAM (St Giles), Church in Wales   *Wrex.*

Location: in town centre.
Access: open daily, 10 a.m.–4 p.m.

This magnificent fifteenth-century church, with its exceptionally handsome west tower, is one of the finest in Wales. Well restored by Benjamin Ferrey in 1866–7, it retains a lectern of 1524, a chancel screen of 1707, fragmentary remains of a doom painting over the chancel arch and an impressive mix of good quality nineteenth- and twentieth-century furnishings, together with a large collection of eighteenth- and nineteenth-century wall tablets. The furnishings include the reredos, rails and marble flooring in the chancel by Sir T. G. Jackson (1914), the pulpit by Ferrey and stained glass by Gibbs (1867), Clayton and Bell (1895) and Powell's (1914). The windows in the south aisle date from between 1892 and 1920 and were all made by the firm of Kempe and Co. The monuments include those to Anne Fryer (d.1817) by Sir Richard Westmacott and one by Roubiliac of 1751–2 to Mary Myddleton.

NY

95. WREXHAM/WRECSAM (Cathedral of Our Lady of Dolours), Roman Catholic   *Wrex.*

Location: in town centre.
Access: open daily, 9 a.m.–6 p.m.

This is the finest of the three Roman Catholic cathedrals in Wales. It was built in 1857 at the expense of Richard Thompson, ironmaster and colliery owner, and designed by Edward Welby Pugin (son of A. W. N.). It became the cathedral of the new diocese of Menevia in 1907 and now serves as that of the Wrexham diocese following the division of the diocese of Menevia and erection of a new cathedral for that diocese at St Joseph's, Swansea. The furnishings are simple but of good quality, the post-Vatican reordering of the sanctuary has been sensitive to the needs of the building, and the whole interior is light and spacious.

NY

3

Churches and Chapels in North-West Wales

96. ABERDARON (St Hywyn), Church in Wales   *Gwyn. (C)*

Location: next to the shore at the end of the B4413 at the far end of the Llŷn peninsula, 14 miles south-west of Nefyn.
Access: open daily, in summer, 10 a.m.–6 p.m. and in winter, 10 a.m.–4 p.m.

The medieval church was abandoned in 1841 when a new building to replace it was erected in the upper part of the village. This is an Italian Romanesque design with twin west towers which retains its original furnishings intact and is maintained by the community council but with unfortunately very limited access to its splendid interior. After its abandonment St Hywyn's was used for twenty years as the premises of the village school which had been established in 1835. During the 1860s the decision was taken to abandon the new church and to return to St Hywyn's, which had been fully repaired by 1868. Situated spectacularly, precipitously, overlooking the sea, St Hywyn's is the westernmost of the major churches of the Llŷn peninsula. It has a special relationship with Bardsey Island (Ynys Enlli) and the poet R. S. Thomas (vicar 1967–78).

The church is of twin nave structure. The northern half was built in the twelfth century and dates from the time when Aberdaron was a *clas* church. A blocked door into the chancel on the north side and changes to the roofline mark the extension of the church in the thirteenth century. The southern half of the church was added in the fifteenth century. A fine Romanesque door in the northern half of the west front gives entry to a light and spacious interior, used both for worship and as a reception area for visitors and pilgrims. There is a plain medieval font of uncertain date. A medieval stoup, recovered from the churchyard, stands inside the door. The restoration of the 1860s unfortunately involved the loss of the medieval screen and choir stalls. In the north-east corner of the church two c. sixth-century ECMs relocated from nearby Capel Anelog record the burials of early churchmen: 'VERACIUS PRESBYTER HIC IACIT' ('Veracius the priest lies here') and 'SENACUS PR[E]SB[YTER] HIC IACIT CVM MVLTITVD[I]NEM FRATRVM' ('Senacus the priest lies here with a large number of his brethren'). The latter is evidence that the monastic life in the western part of Llŷn has a very long tradition.

JW

97. AMLWCH (Our Lady Star of the Sea and St Winefride), Roman Catholic
Angl.

Location: in town centre.
Access: the church is currently closed for a major restoration but it will be generally accessible once the restoration has been completed.

This most unusual church was built in 1932–7. Its architect was Giuseppe Rinvolucri (1894–1963), a civil engineer from Piedmont who moved to north Wales with his English wife c. 1930 because she had tuberculosis. His two other churches in Wales, at Porthmadog and Abergele, are fairly conventional, but Amlwch is not. It is constructed of six reinforced concrete parabolic arches, set on a concrete ring-beam above the masonry parish hall. The west front is also built of stone. All the windows are in the form of stars – a large one over the door, five small ones around the altar recess (which is a 'halved hollow parabolic cone') and bands of prismatic glazing between the ribs of the vault. The lower parts of the walls are lined with coloured marble panels, but the fittings are not worthy of the building. The original altar was replaced in 1995. Structural problems have led to the closure of the church for worship, and its ultimate future use remains to be decided. It must be saved: Ken Powell has written that 'no Catholic church (nor any church of another denomination) built in Britain between the wars has the frankly radical character of Amlwch'. In the porch, a sepulchral slab, mid- to late thirteenth century.

PH

98. BANGOR (St Deiniol's Cathedral), Church in Wales   *Gwyn. (C)*

Location: in city centre.
Access: open daily, 9 a.m.–5 p.m.

The diocese of Bangor is traditionally the oldest in Britain, founded by St Deiniol in the early sixth century. After a Viking raid in 1073, the cathedral was rebuilt under Gruffydd ap Cynan and Bishop David. When the town of Bangor was burned around 1211, the building may have been badly damaged for it was almost entirely rebuilt during the thirteenth and fourteenth centuries. Further work was carried out in the fifteenth century and the tower was added at the west end in 1532.

A huge programme of restoration was instigated by Sir George Gilbert Scott in 1868–70, and continued in 1879–80 by one of his sons, John Oldrid Scott. The east window is by Clayton and Bell (1873) and three windows in the nave are by David Evans of Shrewsbury (1838). The wooden Mostyn Christ is a rare example of a pre-Reformation 'bound rood'. The fourteenth-century Eva stone was discovered below the chapter-room floor in 1879, and is a fine memorial to one Eva, whose family came from near Prestatyn and were generous benefactors to churches on Anglesey. Stones, undoubtedly by the same carver, can be seen at Llanbabo and Llaniestyn churches. In the exhibition area, there are some good fourteenth-century floor tiles and sundry eleventh-century stones with interlace decoration. The Bishop Henry Rowlands Almshouses, north of the church, date from 1805.

AV

99. BARMOUTH/ABERMAW (St John the Evangelist), Church in Wales
Gwyn. (M)

Location: in town centre.
Access: normally open 9 a.m.–4 p.m.

Completed in 1895, St John's is one of the finest and most substantial examples of the ecclesiastical work of Douglas and Fordham, architects from Chester. It sits majestically above the town and is best viewed from the sea front. The exterior is well balanced in its composition which reaches a climax with its lead-spired tower above the crossing. Inside, the space is imposing. High-quality woodwork is a characteristic of this firm's *oeuvre*, and here can be seen good solid pews and a handsome roof structure over the nave, giving an atmosphere which is as much Arts and Crafts as Victorian. The font at the west end is a fine piece of marble work by Davidson & Co. of Inverness (1894) and is a copy of the famous one by Thorvaldsen in Copenhagen Cathedral. There are good windows at the east end by Kempe and the lectern is by Singer of Frome. The church was in large part financed by Mrs F. S. Perrins as a memorial to her late husband, James Dyson Perrins (of Worcestershire Sauce fame). Her generosity extended a second time when the nearly completed tower and much of the remainder of the church collapsed – probably due to faulty footings – and had to be rebuilt. The church hall below the church may be by Douglas and Fordham. Plas Mynach, where Mrs Perrins lived, is the castle-like mansion set on a crag between the sea and the main road north out of Barmouth.

AV

100. BEAUMARIS (St Mary and St Nicholas), Church in Wales   *Angl.*

Location: in town centre.
Access: Open daily, in summer, 9 a.m.–5 p.m., and in winter, 9 a.m.–3.30 p.m.

Built around 1330–40, the church was located near the wall at the western side of the new town. The nave, aisles and tower are of this date. The chancel is probably later, but its walls may be coeval with the fourteenth-century chancel arch. The battlemented parapets and crocketted pinnacles are c.1500. The east windows to the aisles are early sixteenth century and the upper north windows in the chancel are c.1600. Restoration work, which included the removal of galleries in the aisles, reflooring in concrete, replacement of the pews and other furnishings, was carried out by G. F. Bodley in 1902.

The church has some important fittings and memorials. In the porch sits a thirteenth-century coffin and lid, of Joan, daughter of King John and consort of Llywelyn ap Iorwerth. Next to it, a watchman's box, used for guarding the churchyard against body-snatchers in the early nineteenth century. In the north aisle, a fine alabaster tomb commemorates William Bulkeley and his wife, Ellen Gruffydd. The choir stalls and particularly fine misericords are c.1500 and fragments of glass in the south window to the sanctuary range from the same date to the early seventeenth century. Interesting wall memorials are in abundance throughout the church, including (in the chancel) a Roman bust of Thomas Bulkeley by Sir Richard Westmacott and brasses to Richard and Elizabeth Bulkeley, c.1530. Good stained glass by Clayton and Bell (east window) and Kempe.

AV

101. BEDDGELERT (St Mary), Church in Wales   *Gwyn. (C)*

Location: in village centre.

Access: generally open.

A Celtic monastic community was founded here in the sixth century and it was still in existence during Gerald of Wales's travels in 1188. It then became an Augustinian priory. It is uncertain whether any of the twelfth-century church still survives; however, evidence of work carried out around 1230 is far stronger, and it is this work that offers the greatest reward for a visit: the east window, the two-bay arcade between nave and north chapel and the pointed doorway in the north side of the chancel. The triple-lancet east window is stunning, and is best viewed outside from the riverside walk which leads to Gelert's Grave.

The church became the parish church soon after 1538. Later rebuilding in the nineteenth century has hidden or removed much of the evidence of how the church related to the conventual buildings, but it seems that there was a north aisle until well into the eighteenth century, and there was building on the south side too. The south wall of the nave and chancel was rebuilt in 1830 – old carved woodwork and stained glass were removed and sold in order to finance this work! Fifty years later, the north transept was built, the chancel arch was inserted and the bellcote and porch were added at the west end. The oak screens date from 1921.

AV

102. BETWS-Y-COED (St Mary), Church in Wales   *Conwy*

Location: in village centre.
Access: generally open.

St Mary's was designed by Paley and Austin of Lancaster and built in 1870–3 to replace the old church of St Michael's, which still stands to this day, but on another site between the station and the river. What is pleasing about the new church is its architectural composition, both inside and out. The steep roofs of the nave and side aisles neatly contain what is in fact a huge space inside, and the south transept roof cascades almost to ground level. There is handsome blind arcading on the south side of the tower and, instead of the north transept, a semicircular stair turret with conical roof. Inside, the proportions are most satisfactory and the detailing competently designed in Transitional Norman style and carried out using pink Ancaster stone. There is something intriguing about a crossing that is only half a crossing – seen from the south-west, with no north transept built, it is more like a double chancel. The nave and clerestory windows form little arched alcoves – a nice touch.

The fixtures and fittings are all of a piece, and there is some good Victorian stained glass. The west windows in both aisles are by Morris & Co. (1919), and there are some by Shrigley and Hunt (1915). Particularly attractive is the easternmost window in the north wall of the north aisle, either by Edward Burne-Jones or in his style. The pews are good, too, especially the Arts and Crafts choir stalls. The parish hall, triangular in section, was added in 1978.

AV

103. BETWS-Y-COED (St Michael), formerly Church in Wales, now vested in a local trust
Conwy

Location: towards the east end of the village and opposite the railway station.
Access: key available from Railway Museum, daily, 10 a.m.–4.45 p.m.

The original church consisting of undivided nave and chancel is fourteenth or fifteenth century. The two-centred arched doorway on the south side of the church is the chief feature of this date. Inside, the arched niche and effigy of Gruffydd ap Dafydd Goch, at the north-east corner, is also of this date. In 1843, a major transformation took place under the patronage of Lord Willoughby de Eresby of Gwydir. Most of the north wall was removed and an unusually wide transept was added, with benches all facing the double-decker pulpit on the south wall, reassembled from pieces of sixteenth- and seventeenth-century material. Then, or later, the roof structure was concealed above a plain plaster barrel-vaulted ceiling, and the windows were 'modernised' and given quirky pointed tops. What is interesting about this little church is the way the medieval building was radically altered in the early Victorian era as a result of changing liturgical requirements. The uncompromising nature of the alterations is now part of the building's historical development and can be admired as such.

AV

104. BRITHDIR (St Mark), formerly Church in Wales, now cared for by the Friends of Friendless Churches
Gwyn. (M)

Location: on a side road between the A470 and the A494, 2 miles east of Dolgellau.
Access: generally open.

Mrs Charles Tooth built this church in memory of her second husband, founder of St Mark's Anglican Church in Florence. Her architect was

Henry Wilson, formerly senior assistant of John Dando Sedding, and a designer of remarkable originality, best known for his metalwork. Built in 1895–7, St Mark's is without doubt one of the finest Arts and Crafts churches in Britain. Wilson told Mrs Tooth that the church should look 'as if it had sprung out of the soil instead of being planted on it . . . I have built it as simply as I know how'. It was essential that local materials should be used, hence the granite and slates. Wilson would no doubt have been horrified to see the church surrounded by yews and rhododendrons, as it is now. It is cruciform in plan. The broad west gable, with the roof sweeping down over porches with battered walls, is striking. The interior comes as a surprise. The lofty cream-painted nave contrasts with the barrel-vaulted and apsed chancel, which is decorated in dark red, pale green and pale blue (the colours perhaps not quite accurately renewed). Wilson looked forward to 'embellishing the interior in an individual and country manner'. The lovely altar, with its cast copper front showing the Annunciation, was given by Charles Tooth's brother Arthur, the first Anglican priest imprisoned for ritualism. The pulpit is also copper, and the font, modelled by Arthur Grove, of lead. The stalls are carved with animals, and the doors inlaid with mother-of-pearl. Note the door handles.

PH

105. BRYNYMAEN (Christ Church), Church in Wales   *Conwy*

Location: on the B5113, 2 miles north of Colwyn Bay.
Access: service on Sundays at 9.30 a.m.

A local girl, Eleanor Jones, vowed that if she became rich she would build a church. She went into service with the Frosts of Colwyn Bay, married the heir and, in 1897–8, duly built church, vicarage and a house for herself in her hilltop village. Her architects were Douglas and Fordham, who had built St Paul's Church in Colwyn Bay. Christ Church is a surprisingly sophisticated and expensive building to find on its upland site, to which its toughness is well suited. It has a low, battlemented tower over the choir, a short chancel and low transepts. The style is Perpendicular. The exterior is of local limestone, but the interior is lined with warm red Helsby sandstone. The broad nave has a hammerbeam roof, and the east window is framed by the wide tower arches. The rich wooden fittings are characteristic of Douglas, including even the hymn board, almsbox and umbrella stand. This is one of Douglas's most felicitous creations.

PH

106. CAERDEON/BONTDDU (St Philip), Church in Wales *Gwyn. (M)*

Location: on the A496, 3 miles north-east of Barmouth.
Access: generally open.

12. Caerdeon/Bontddu, St Philip. © Crown copyright: *Royal Commission on the Ancient and Historical Monuments of Wales*

This extraordinary church was built in 1862 as the result of a dispute between the Revd W. E. Jelf, who coached undergraduates in Classics here, and the rector of Llanaber, who refused to provide English services. After it was built, the rector cited a law of Queen Elizabeth's time according to which services in predominantly Welsh areas had to be in Welsh. As a result, in 1863 the English Services in Wales Act was passed, providing that services could be in English if ten or more parishioners requested them. As built, the church consisted of a rectangular building of rough local stone, with plain rectangular windows and a rough loggia over the entrance, on square piers. It has broad eaves, and a circular window at what was the sanctuary end. A tablet over the door commemorates Jelf's father-in-law, the Revd John Petit, 'founder and benefactor'. He was well known as an amateur archaeologist, watercolour painter and author of books on church architecture illustrated with his sketches. In designing Caerdeon he took his lead from Alpine mountain chapels, but *The Ecclesiologist* (journal of the Ecclesiological Society) was not impressed, describing the church as 'something between a large lodge gate and a lady's rustic dairy'.

PH

107. CEFNCYMERAU (Capel Salem), Baptist   *Gwyn. (M)*

Location: off the A496 on the eastern outskirts of Llanbedr, 3 miles south of Harlech.
Access: generally open.

This chapel was made famous by the painting of its interior by Curnow Vosper. It was built in 1850 and extended in 1860. The pulpit is on one of the short walls with the communion pew below it. Seating is provided by box pews, tiered towards the short wall opposite the pulpit. There are hat pegs along all four walls, including on the pulpit backboard. Baptisms take place in the stream beside the chapel.

NY

108. CLYNNOG FAWR (St Beuno), Church in Wales   *Gwyn. (C)*

Location: on the A499 between Caernarfon and Pwllheli.
Access: generally open.

St Beuno's is one of the finest and most important churches in north-west Wales. A *clas* church which adopted collegiate status after the conquest, it was the main shrine of St Beuno and remained a centre of pilgrimage up to the Reformation.

The plan is a cruciform, with a west tower and, joined to this by a tunnel-like passage, a chapel. The chancel and transepts date from around 1480, the nave and porch around 1500, the three-storey vestry block, tower and chapel all early sixteenth century and the passage early seventeenth century. Various alterations were made later, but none that fundamentally changed this remarkably consistent example of late Perpendicular architecture.

The whitewashed interior is a haven of peace, uncluttered with benches and other Victorian fittings, and gloriously awash with daylight (not a single window contains stained glass). One unusual feature is the way the roofs of the transepts continue through, uninterrupted by the nave roof. Fittings of note are the seventeenth-century screen to the tower archway, the restored chancel screen and choir stalls (early sixteenth century), the sedilia and adjacent piscina in the chancel, a pair of dog-tongs in the south transept, Beuno's Chest (in a glass case at the front of the nave), formed from a single piece of ash, and numerous memorials (the most touching is in the north-east corner of the chancel, dated 1609, to William Glynne of Lleuar, and shows an obedient family of ten daughters and two sons kneeling behind an adult, like ducklings following their mother).

AV

13. Clynnog Fawr, St Beuno. *Adam Voelcker*

109. CONWY (St Mary and All Saints), Church in Wales   *Conwy*

Location: in town centre.
Access: Mondays–Fridays in summer, 10 a.m.–12 p.m. and 2 p.m.–4 pm.

Located in the heart of the walled town and with access by alleyways on all four sides, St Mary and All Saints is an important church showing work of many periods. It was part of the Cistercian abbey of Aberconwy founded by monks who moved from Strata Florida in 1186.

The earliest surviving remnants of the church are parts of the west wall, including the triple lancets above the west door and possibly the lower parts of the east end of the chancel (*c.*1190–1220). The original church may have been in the cruciform plan typical of monastic churches, or perhaps it remained unfinished. After 1282, the nave, aisles and parts of the chancel were rebuilt, and the tower was inserted into the west bay of the nave; a vestry was added on the north side of the chancel. In the early fourteenth century, the south transept was built – a fine piece of work (though the south window and roof are later) whose quality contrasts with the remainder of the church, possibly because it was built by English masons. Later still are the two porches, the top stage of the tower and the parish room north of the tower (formerly a charnel house). The roof over the nave and side aisles was previously in one sweep each side, but in 1872 Sir George Gilbert Scott raised the nave roof by inserting clerestory walls. In 1926, the vestry was extended northwards.

The church contains fine features and fittings. Best of all is perhaps the chancel screen (*c.*1500) even though it has been much changed over the years. It may have come from Ludlow originally, and had higher parapets to accommodate musicians (access was from a stair and doorway still visible in the south transept). The carving is lovely and contains Tudor roses, pomegranates, vine scrolls, the Black Prince's feathers and assorted beasts. Parts of the choir stalls are of the same date. The gritstone font is fifteenth century and the tiles set in the south wall of the chancel are fourteenth century or earlier. There are some pretty windows by Edward Burne-Jones in the south aisle and in the parish room two panels of lace should not be missed (*c.*1600).

AV

110. DEGANWY (All Saints), Church in Wales   *Conwy*

Location: on the coast road midway between Conwy and Llandudno.
Access: services on Sundays at 8 a.m. and 11 a.m. and on Wednesdays
at 10 a.m.

This picturesque church occupies a superb site overlooking the Conwy estuary. It was built in 1897–9 by Lady Augusta Mostyn, of Gloddaeth, in memory of her parents. Her architects were Douglas and Fordham. At the west end is a stout tower, with a short broach spire, and hipped roofs to the buttresses. The aisled and clerestoried nave climbs up the hill towards the chancel, which is taller. The result is a quirky composition typical of Douglas. The nave and aisles are lined with tooled rubble, but the chancel with ashlar. The detailing of the nave arcade shows (in Edward Hubbard's words) 'extreme trickiness'. The wooden furnishings incorporate miniature turned balusters and posts with ball finials. The reredos dates from 1905. Much of the stained glass (east and west windows, east window of south aisle, baptistery windows) is by Lavers and Westlake.

PH

111. DOLGELLAU (St Mary), Church in Wales   *Gwyn. (M)*

Location: in town centre.
Access: open daily, 8.30 a.m.–5.30 p.m.

Eighteenth-century churches are rare in north Wales, and this is one of the few, built in 1716 to replace an earlier church of which there is no record. What makes the church remarkable apart from its date is the quality of its construction, all carried out in classical style, but one which has also grown from the granite character of Dolgellau. The huge blocks of stone are so regular that hardly a mortar joint shows, and the blocks to the apsidal sanctuary (added in 1864) are gently curved. The huge windows have classical semicircular heads and the jambs are formed with bold projecting quoins. At external angles, the corner stones interlock with each other, a detail as fine as it is unique in this region.

The interior is spacious and of a character quite unlike other churches in north Wales. The ceiling is vast, a shallow barrel-vault of dark stained timber supported on tall thin wooden columns. The sanctuary apse is mirrored at the west end by the wall to the new accommodation added in 1992. Notice the round-headed windows, the continuation of the heavy timber cornice and the skilful way the dividing wall respects the columns – designed by local architect Roy Olsen, it is an exercise in good architectural manners.

The only medieval remnant is the effigy of Meurig ab Ynyr Fychan, c.1345. Outside, in the churchyard, is a large collection of seventeenth- and eighteenth-century gravestones interspersed amongst the yew trees, and beyond the churchyard walls, the handsome stone houses of Dolgellau connected by a web of narrow lanes and alleys.

AV

112. DOLWYDDELAN (St Gwyddelan), Church in Wales   *Conwy*

Location: in village on A470, 6 miles south-west of Betws-y-Coed.
Access: generally open during the summer.

As with so many Welsh churches, the treasures that St Gwyddelan's boasts are hidden behind a plain, almost featureless, exterior. A rugged roof of *cerrig mwsog* (rough slates with moss between) protects equally rugged walls built of large stones. Particularly crude, but no less fine, are the monolithic lintels above the two east windows and the main entrance door. The oversized gable crosses are Victorian, as are the south and west windows, the porch and the bellcote – all the work of Lord Willoughby de Eresby around 1850. The main part of the church was built around 1500 by Maredudd ap Ieuan; the south chapel was added by Robert Wynn of Plas Mawr, Conwy, much later in the same century.

The interior of the main body of the church is divided into two halves as a result of the added chapel. This is because the oak screen was originally further east and separated the sanctuary from the rest of the church in the traditional manner, with a rood loft above. The northernmost compartment was filled with latticework, probably forming a simple confessional. The eighteenth-century balustrade at the top of the screen was put there around 1850 – until then, it had formed the front of a gallery at the west end of the nave. The junction of the chapel with the nave is formed by a pair of semicircular arches supported on a rough cylindrical pillar – an unusual feature that Sir Stephen Glynne thought most ugly when he visited the church in 1850, but one which would warrant further research. Could it be Roman, and have originated at the camp at Caerhun?

The roofs are supported on oak arch-braced trusses, filled between in the chancel to form a ceiling. Notice the carved dragon on the coving to this ceiling above the north window. Other items of interest are the small brass plaques set behind glass on the north wall (early sixteenth century); next to these, a Jacobean mural monument to the Wynn family; an early medieval bronze hand-bell; fragments of medieval glass set in the chancel windows (c.1500); the unusual eighteenth-century pews with slatted backs and scalloped entrances and the poor box hollowed out of an oak beam.

AV

113. GLANYRAFON/LLAWR Y BETWS (Christ Church), Church in Wales   *Gwyn. (M)*

Location: by itself on the A494, 4 miles south-west of Corwen.
Access: service on Sundays at 11 a.m.

This simple Early English church was built in 1861–4 as a memorial to Sir Robert and Lady Williams-Vaughan of Rûg, who died before they could build it. Nave and chancel are under one roof, with a bellcote over the chancel arch. Although not large, the church is a good example of Scott's ability to give a plain building dignity and character. The glass in the east window is by O'Connor, and the font is of Caen stone, but the finest feature of the interior is the splendid tiled reredos, by Minton.

PH

114. GWYDIR UCHAF (Holy Trinity), private chapel, now in the custody of Cadw
Conwy

Location: off the B5106, 1 mile south-west of Llanrwst and signposted from main road.
Access: key held by Mr and Mrs Peter Welford, telephone: 01492 641687.

The chapel was built in 1673 and preserves its magnificent contemporary painted ceiling and west gallery. The eighteenth-century furnishings comprise the three-sided altar rails, seats for communicants, stalls along the north and south walls and chairs in the middle of the central space. The pulpit is placed in the middle of the southern block of stalls with the reading desk, returned and facing east, at the west end of the same block.

NY

115. GYFFIN (St Benedict), Church in Wales
Conwy

Location: in the southern outskirts of Conwy.
Access: service on Sundays at 9.30 a.m.

This small late medieval church was made a T-plan in the post-Reformation period through the addition of north and south transepts to the chancel. Although heavily restored in the nineteenth century it retains a medieval font and a magnificent fifteenth-century roof over both nave and chancel. Over the east end of the chancel is a superb canopy of honour, comprising sixteen painted panels with figures of the twelve apostles and the four evangelical symbols. The altar rails date from the eighteenth century and there is a handsome seventeenth-century parish chest.

NY

116. HOLYHEAD/CAERGYBI (St Cybi), Church in Wales   *Angl.*

Location: in town centre.
Access: normally June–August, 10 a.m.–3 p.m.

On the site of a monastery founded by St Cybi in *c*.550 the oldest part of the extant church is the chancel, which although rebuilt and with a Victorian roof, is thirteenth century. Extensive work was carried out in the late fifteenth to early sixteenth centuries and is contemporary with Clynnog Fawr church and the chancel at Beaumaris church: the two transepts were added *c*.1480, the north aisle *c*.1500 and the south aisle and porch *c*.1520. The finely carved parapet to the south transept is probably of this third phase, as is the exuberant south doorway with its decoratively carved panels above, although the fan-vaulting above is of 1877–9. The tower is probably seventeenth century. The Victorians had their turn and carried out work in two phases: first, a comprehensive restoration by Sir George Gilbert Scott in 1877–9 and later the addition of the south (Stanley) chapel by his former pupil/assistant Arthur Baker in 1896–7.

The interior has a spacious and lofty quality, helped in large part by the unusually tall piers of the south arcade. Points of interest include: two stone fonts of 1662 and twelfth century (the latter moved from Llanfair-yn-Neubwll church); the painted Tudor rose on the east wall of the north transept (late fifteenth century); the organ (Whiteley of Chester, 1881 – moved from Eaton Hall, Cheshire) and the white Carrara marble Stanley tomb by Hamo Thornycroft. Glass in the main east window is by Kempe, and matching windows in the south chapel and north transept were designed by Burne-Jones and made by Morris & Co. The south-east window in the chapel is less good (by a number of different lesser-known designers) but the pomegranate window above the Stanley tomb is lovely, and is as refreshing as it is unusual for its lack of human figures.

The Eglwys y Bedd, beside the south gateway into the churchyard, is the nave of a fourteenth-century chapel. The blocked archway one sees above the entrance is the original chancel arch. The building was used as a school in the eighteenth century.

AV

117. LLANABER (St Mary and St Bodfan), Church in Wales *Gwyn. (M)*

Location: on the A496 about 1 mile north of Barmouth Park in the lay-by near the lychgate.
Access: generally open.

One of a number of attractive churches along the Meirionnydd coastline, this church has particular significance for its intact Early English architecture. The original church was founded by St Bodfan in the sixth century, but was rebuilt in the early thirteenth century by Hywel ap Gruffydd ap Cynan, a benefactor of Cymer Abbey. The massive Norman arcade piers and rounded arches of Tywyn church have here developed into a new more sophisticated style not before seen in this part of Wales. See how the capitals also develop, from rather primitive petals on the arcade piers to glorious (but sadly weather-worn) stiff-leaf foliage on the fine entrance archway, surely one of the best church doorways in north Wales. The heavily structured oak roofs are later (c.1500), culminating in a wagon-roof ceiling above the sanctuary. In 1858, the church underwent a careful restoration, when a new porch was built, a vestry replaced the chapel on the north side of the chancel and the west gable and bellcote were rebuilt. Some of the windows were rebuilt recently.

Fittings include a fifteenth-century octagonal font carved with quatrefoils and heraldic shields, a thirteenth-century graveslab in the nave, two late fifth- or early sixth-century inscribed stones hidden away at the back of the north aisle and an attractive early twentieth-century reredos. Best of all, though, is the tranquil and unspoilt quality of the interior space – and the setting beside the sea matches it.

AV

118. LLANAELHAEARN (St Aelhaearn), Church in Wales *Gwyn. (C)*

Location: in the old part of the village between the A499 and the B4417, 6 miles north-east of Nefyn.
Access: details on notice board.

A cruciform church with twelfth-century nave, sixteenth-century north transept, south transept probably of 1622 and a Victorian chancel and vestry. The former chancel extended only about 1.5 metres beyond the transepts, had a boarded ceiling and was joined to the chancel without arches (the screen was at this time west of the crossing). In 1848, Henry Kennedy restored the church and beautified the crossing by inserting some arches but, by 1892 when the church was restored again, the arches were removed and the chancel was lengthened to its present size. The reset east window is fourteenth century and its form, with three lights and simple deep reveals, is reminiscent of the east window in Beddgelert church.

The interior of the church is perhaps of more interest than the rather plain exterior. The first thing to strike one on entering is the elegant array of pews with turned balusters in the doors and seat backs. These date from the mid-nineteenth century. The oak screen is fifteenth century and the pulpit eighteenth century. The Aliortus stone is fifth or sixth century and was discovered in a field in 1865. In translation, it reads 'Aliortus a man of Elmet lies here' – a long way from home, which was then a kingdom of its own, now a suburb of Leeds. The other inscribed stone to notice is just inside the churchyard gate, on the right, to Melitus. It is quite likely that this is in its original position.

AV

119. LLANBEDROG (St Petroc), Church in Wales   *Gwyn. (C)*

Location: turn south at service station on A499 before the main village; church is on the hill to the right; limited parking.
Access: generally open during the summer.

Easily overlooked in the old village south of the main road, this beautiful medieval church is dedicated to a Cornish saint. The church is a simple rectangle. Entrance is via a porch in the base of the tower. Nave and chancel are under one roof: the nave is thirteenth century, the chancel an extension of the early sixteenth century. The tower was added in the nineteenth century. The beautiful screen and west window are medieval.

JW

120. LLANDANWG (St Tanwg), Church in Wales   *Gwyn. (C)*

Location: off the A496, 2 miles south-west of Harlech.
Access: service on the third Sunday of the month (every Sunday in late July and August) at 6.30 p.m.

Almost hidden amongst the sand dunes which threaten to overwhelm it, Llandanwg is a simple, unspoilt, medieval church. The abandonment of the church after the building of a new church in Harlech saw the interior escape the changes of the Gothic revival. The church is a single-cell structure of late medieval date with plastered timber barrel roof and white-painted rough-cast walls. The rood beam is still in place above the nave. A single row of bench pews spans almost the width of the nave. The east window in three lights is Perpendicular in style. Two ECMs (c. sixth century) are in the chancel. One reads 'EQVESTRINOMINE' (the person named Equester [lies here]), the other 'IN[G]ENVI IARRI[-- HI]C IA[CIT]' ('[the stone of] Ingenuus Iarrus. He lies here'). The church was restored to use in 1884. The claim, first made in the eighteenth century, that the church was a staging point for Bardsey Island (Ynys Enlli) is unverifiable, but Bardsey is a constant presence on the other side of Tremadog Bay.

JW

121. LLANDDERFEL (St Derfel), Church in Wales   *Gwyn. (M)*

Location: in village on the B4402, 4 miles north-east of Bala.
Access: key at Tirionfa (nursing home further up the hill, on right-hand side).

Sitting in a quiet little village surrounded by wooded hills, Llandderfel church owes its modest fame to a wooden effigy. One theory is that it is a horse and once had a wooden figure of Derfel riding it, but in 1538 he was removed by Cromwell's men and taken to London to be burnt. The animal stayed put and now sits in the porch.

The church itself is unremarkable, except that it is unusual to find in Meirionnydd a medieval church of this late date (*c.*1500). It is well constructed with long rectangular stones, superior to random rubble stonework, a reflection, perhaps, of the popularity of St Derfel with pilgrims who no doubt helped finance the construction. The windows are of dressed stone, with four-centred heads, simple Perpendicular tracery and carved stops to the hood moulds – animals and human heads, some quite grotesque. The porches were added in 1639, and the church was restored in 1870 by S. Pountney Smith of Shrewsbury, who was involved with the building of nearby Palé Hall.

A further treasure inside is the oak screen which divides the chancel from the nave. It has four bays each side of a central doorway, and the head of each has little foliated embellishments. The head beam is finely decorated with vine trails and pomegranates, and above is part of the original loft which served time as a gallery front at the west end before being returned to the screen. The reredos was also part of the rood loft and is a good example of mid-fifteenth-century work.

AV

122. LLANDDOGED (St Doged), Church in Wales *Conwy*

Location: in village off A548, 2 miles north of Llanrwst.
Access: key is at house opposite church gate.

The exterior of this church is hardly of interest. Partly rebuilt in 1838–9, it is said to be the collaborative effort of two local vicars without the help of an architect. But the interior is far more rewarding as it is a fine example of a pre-ecclesiological layout unspoilt by Victorian churchmen and their architects. Instead of uniform rows of benches all facing east, the layout is a busy landscape of box pews seemingly facing all directions, making it hard to see where the liturgical focus is. The communion table is, in fact, where one would expect, but the pulpit rises high above the pews halfway along the north wall. It is a two-decker affair, or three if one counts the detached clerk's desk in front. All the pew compartments have doors and are numbered. The back ones are tight and narrow, the most comfortable (east end of the south aisle) is spacious and has upholstered padding to the seats and backs. Children sat in the tiered benches at the west end, boys on the left, girls on the right. So unspoilt is this interior, one can almost visualise the church full, with its hierarchy of local parishioners.

AV

123. LLANDWROG (St Twrog), Church in Wales   *Gwyn. (C)*

Location: in centre of village off A499, 6 miles south-west of Caernarfon.
Access: generally open.

Churches with tall spires are a rarity in north Wales, so St Twrog's is an exception and a very fine one at that. Paid for by the third Lord Newborough and built in 1858–64 as an integral part of the estate village of Llandwrog, it was designed in the Decorated style by the diocesan architect Henry Kennedy and, maybe because the budget was ample, he was able to achieve what is arguably his best work. The most interesting feature is the interior layout, formed in high Victorian collegiate style with the stalls in the nave and north transept all facing in towards the centre. The gallery at the west end accommodates the organ and is constructed, unusually, of stone. Other features of note are the iron chancel screen, a good Clayton and Bell window in the north transept, some early to mid-eighteenth-century memorials from the previous church and a monument to Sir Thomas Wynn (d.1749), perhaps by Sir Henry Cheere, and to members of the Bodvell family of Bodfan, by Joseph Nollekens. The lychgate is a fine essay in its own right and, with the avenue of yews along the pathway, forms a grand approach to an exceptional church.

AV

124. LLANDYGAI (St Tygai), Church in Wales   *Gwyn. (C)*

Location: follow the old A5 just past the main gateway to Penrhyn Castle, then turn left through the wall into the village of Llandygai; the church is at the end of the lane.
Access: open on Wednesdays and Saturdays in summer, 10 a.m.– 6 p.m.

Although Penrhyn Castle has its own chapel, St Tygai's served as the church of the Pennant family as well as the surrounding parish and has something of an estate feel about it. Set within the picturesque model village of Llandygai, access to the church is along a fine avenue of yews and iron railings.

Very little remains of the original church. To this was added in the sixteenth century the chancel, the two transepts and the tower; the tower was rebuilt in 1853 as was most of the nave (which was also lengthened). A gallery and porch were added at the west end, and battlemented parapets were introduced at roof level – all the work of Henry Kennedy, diocesan architect.

Inside there are three fine monuments. The fifteenth-century alabaster altar tomb at the west end may have been erected for Sir William Griffith of Penrhyn (d.1490). The wall monument on the south side of the chancel commemorates Archbishop John Williams (d.1650) who was appointed archbishop of York by Charles I and had local connections with the Penrhyn and Cochwillan families. The most elaborate of the three is the Penrhyn memorial on the north side of the chancel (1821, by R. Westmacott, RA), all in white marble. In the churchyard, to the south-east of the chancel, is a large pyramidal tomb to Benjamin Wyatt, architect to the Penrhyn estate as well as other buildings in the area.

AV

125. LLANDYGWNNING (St Iestyn), formerly Church in Wales, now in the care of a local trust)   *Gwyn. (C)*

Location: by itself off the B4413, 8 miles west of Pwllheli.
Access: generally open during the summer and at weekends during the winter; key holder lives adjacent to the church.

This dear little toy church, perfectly suited to its rustic Llŷn setting, was built in 1840 to the design of John Welch of St Asaph – an architect blissfully unaware of current archaeological and liturgical scholarship. It has a circular tower and conical spire, with a slate sundial. The simple nave has windows with wooden tracery. The interior is fitted with box pews and a two-decker pulpit. There is a good tablet of 1721 to Jane Jones.

PH

126. LLANEGRYN (St Egryn), Church in Wales   *Gwyn. (M)*

Location: by itself off the A493, 4 miles north-east of Tywyn.
Access: generally open.

A tranquil spot, which is noted not for the unremarkable church itself but for the gem inside – the sixteenth-century screen and rood loft. The screen is situated between the nave and chancel, thus forming a division between the two spaces otherwise not possible in a single-cell church. It consists of three open bays each side of a central doorway. Projecting out above is the loft, from which singers and musicians would have provided music before the day of the organ. Above the screen, a rood (cross) would have been displayed. The carving both sides is sumptuous. Particularly fine are the seventeen panels on the east face. Also worth noting are the arch-braced roof structure, the font (possibly twelfth century) and the eighteenth-century memorials to members of the Peniarth family, located in the chancel.

AV

127. LLANEILIAN (St Eilian), Church in Wales   *Angl.*

Location: on a side road, signed to Point Lynas, off the A5025, 2 miles east of Amlwch.
Access: open May–September, 10 a.m.–4 p.m.

Perhaps one of the finest churches on Anglesey, St Eilian's boasts a twelfth-century tower with pyramid-shaped top (similar to those at Penmon and Puffin Island), and a late fourteenth- or early fifteenth-century chapel connected to the main church around 1614. The nave and chancel were rebuilt in the late fifteenth century over earlier origins. The walls are of local rubble stone, but the parapets and pinnacles are of red sandstone, probably imported and used because it is softer to cut than the local stone. The hidden roofs are leaded, and the present lime finish to the tower replaces nasty mid-twentieth-century pebbledash (and before that, slating) so that once again the church 'glitters like the firmament with stars', as most churches probably did in the time of Gruffudd ap Cynan.

Inside, very fine features include the choir stalls, the rood screen and loft (note the painted skeleton facing the nave), carved corbelled figures at ceiling level and handsome oak work to the chancel and chapel roofs (the new oak boss in the chancel ceiling commemorates extensive repair work carried out in 2002). The chapel is approached via the sanctuary, and contains amongst other artefacts a shrine pedestal worn smooth inside by people ritually turning round three times at the saint's wake. Outside, notice the consecration crosses and lombardic inscriptions (late fifteenth century) cut into the buttresses, and the unusual straight arch heads to the east window.

AV

128. LLANENGAN (St Engan), Church in Wales   *Gwyn. (C)*

Location: the easiest way is to go to Abersoch (A499 south-west from Pwllheli), then follow signs to Llanengan.
Access: key available at Tanyfynwent or Wern (houses along road from Abersoch).

Set in the middle of a quiet village, the church's tower (c.1534) sits at the west end of the earlier of the two aisles. At the east end, the chancel marks the point where the church was probably first extended eastwards around 1520. The church was then enlarged southwards (possibly just in the chancel area first of all, since the arcade piers here are different from those along the nave – they have a close similarity to some found at Llangwnnadl church, dated c.1520). The building of the tower and the south porch (originally two-storey) formed a third phase of this development, and no further changes took place until 1847 when the church was restored by Henry Kennedy, and later, in 1937–8, when there was further restoration.

The interior of the church contains much of interest. Foremost are the pair of early Tudor oak screens and stalls at the east end. The one in the south aisle still retains its loft, and is equal to any in north Wales (cf. Conwy, Llanegryn, Llaneilian). The roof trusses are fine examples of early sixteenth-century work and warrant more than a cursory glance as hardly one is similar to the next (those in the nave, heavier and with wind-braces, may be earlier).

For those who want to discover more, there is an abundance of date inscriptions: look at the sides of the east window, on the eastern arcade pier, over the west doorway to the tower, on some of the roof trusses, even on some of the rainwater heads. There is a memorial of 1721 on the east wall of the south aisle, a fifteenth-century font and a handsome late seventeenth-century communion table just inside the entrance. The east windows contain Kempe glass reset in modern leadwork designed by Donald Buttress, c.1980.

AV

129. LLANFAGLAN (St Mary Magdalene), formerly Church in Wales, now in the care of the Friends of Friendless Churches   Gwyn. (C)

Location: access is through a gate and across a field, off the coastal lane which connects Caernarfon and Llandwrog; no direct access is possible by going west at Llanfaglan crossroads.
Access: kept locked; key available from W. H. Jones (telephone: 01286 831335) or R. Bayles (telephone: 01286 673003).

This church has a magical location. It sits all alone, in a walled churchyard with barley fields all around, facing one way towards the Menai Straits, the other towards the western hills of Snowdonia. It is almost possible (pleasure flights apart) to witness the utter seclusion of some of the remoter churches in earlier times.

The oldest part of the church is the nave and this may have earlier origins than the pointed thirteenth-century door suggests. The south chapel was added in the late sixteenth or early seventeenth century, and the chancel around 1800 (the fourteenth-century east window must have been reset then). The porch was probably built then, too, perhaps reusing timber from the earlier chancel. Despite the few windows, the interior is surprisingly light, mainly because the walls and ceilings, even the roof timbers, are limewashed in a rich cream colour. The collection of eighteenth-century benches and pews is the chief attraction inside: some are open benches with no adornment, others have rounded ends; the box pews are fairly plain, but the best is in oak and has a carved top rail. The double-decker pulpit has a small sounding board above it, and the altar is enclosed on three sides by railings with slender turned balusters. The wall memorials, mostly of slate and also eighteenth century, are charmingly naive in their execution. There are some carved stones which are easily missed: the sill and head of the porch window are thirteenth-century grave slabs with incised crosses (the sill also has a ship), and above the door internally is a reused sixth-century cross inscribed 'FILI LOVERNII / ANATEMORI' ('to Anatemorus, son of Lovernius').

AV

130. LLANFROTHEN (St Brothen), formerly Church in Wales, now in the care of the Friends of Friendless Churches *Gwyn. (M)*

Location: off the A4085; 2 miles north of Penrhyndeudraeth take the B4410 from Garreg-Llanfrothen towards Rhyd; at chapel beyond sharp bend, take lane on right-hand side, leading sharply up towards Llan Farm; park in lane where road widens rather than in farm, and take footpath between the pair of farmhouses. Beware of the dogs.
Access: generally open.

The church was built in the thirteenth century with a continuous nave and chancel; the porch was added much later. The exterior is plain and barn-like, but has a fine triple lancet window at the east end, and the rugged slate roof is entirely in keeping with the landscape (from which the slates will have been dug). Inside, it feels more spacious than the exterior suggests, and the floor rises as you process from nave to chancel. As you go eastwards, notice the late fifteenth-century octagonal font, some seventeenth-century bench ends, the rood screen (ring-dated c.1500) and beam beyond (possibly once part of the rood loft). The carved beam behind the altar, supported on posts with seventeenth-century finials and called 'Y Gredin' (The Creed), was perhaps an upper part of the original screen. One of the memorials in the chancel is to William Williams of Brondanw (d.1778), who built the first sea-banks in the area. The handsome roof trusses are probably fifteenth century, but much else in the roof structure is later.

AV

131. LLANGADWALADR (St Cadwaladr), Church in Wales   *Angl.*

Location: off the A4080 between Newborough and Aberffraw, about
2 miles east of the latter; look for church sign just east of junction with
road to Bethel.

Access: the church is normally open in the summer on Tuesdays,
Thursdays and Fridays; if it is locked details of key holders are displayed
on the notice board.

This is a church whose importance is vastly disproportionate to its
modest size. Here we have architecture, glass, monuments and an
inscribed stone of the highest quality not only in the context of Anglesey
but of north Wales as a whole.

The church was founded by Cadwaladr ap Cadwallon, grandson of
Cadfan ap Iago ap Beli who died c.625. His church was no doubt a
wooden one, built on the site of the royal burial ground associated with
the court at Aberffraw, but the church we see today is stone and a
mixture of much later periods. The nave is essentially late twelfth or early
thirteenth century but the only feature of this date which is obvious is the
blocked doorway in the north wall (the roof and windows are Victorian).
A chancel was added in the fourteenth century, then a pair of chapels was
attached either side of the chancel after the Reformation: the north
chapel by the Meyrick family of Bodorgan (1640) and the south chapel by
Ann Owen in memory of her husband Hugh (1661). The latter is a
wonderfully bright and airy space inside with its large perpendicular-style
clear glass windows. There is a fine monument on the wall above the door,
and next to the door a small window which was reputedly used by lepers
who lived nearby in the seventeenth century. The ceiling in the chapel
was formerly boarded and painted brightly. It seems sad that Hugh Owen
died before he could see his dream built.

The layout, fittings and furnishings inside the church are by Henry
Kennedy (1859) and are of no particular merit. The Cadfan stone set
into the north wall of the nave and the glass in the east window of the
chancel are outstanding, however. The stone commemorates the death
of King Cadfan (Catamanus) and would have stood vertically at the head
of his grave. It reads 'CATAMANUS / REX SAPIENTISI / MUS OPINATISIM /

US OMNIUM REG / UM' ('King Catamanus wisest [and] most renowned of all kings lies here'). The lettering is a mixture of Roman capitals and half-uncials (a style of writing used in manuscripts) and the Celtic cross is believed to be the first ever used on a tombstone. The glass in the east window is fifteenth century and has been reset (the window itself is nineteenth century), providing one of the best and most complete examples of medieval glass in north Wales. Of interest is the way the bones of Christ can be seen as in an X-ray. The two nineteenth-century stained-glass windows in the north chapel are worth a look, too.

AV

132. LLANGELYNNIN (St Celynnin), Church in Wales   *Conwy*

Location: narrow back lanes from Henryd, Conwy or Sychnant; follow signs at top.
Access: generally open.

14. Llangelynnin, St Celynnin. *Adam Voelcker*

This church could hardly be less accessible, and though a modern lane will allow car access within a good stone's throw of the church, it is best approached on foot from the south-east side, up a series of winding wall-lined paths, to appreciate how remote the church is, and what an effort church-going must have been before a new church was built down in the valley.

As so often with these small churches, the nave is the oldest part and although joined to it without division, the chancel is later. The porch may be of this date or later, and the north chapel, Capel y Meibion (the men's chapel), is probably sixteenth century. Foundations outside indicate that there was also a south chapel but this was removed around 1800.

Before entering the church, take time to enjoy the porch: the arch-braced truss, the little oak gates, the squint in the east wall (an unusual location for this and its function is uncertain, but it seems to line up with the churchyard gateway), the fine oak door frame with its high threshold, and take heed of the notice above the door:

'This is a House of God – visitors are requested not to scribble anywhere.'

Inside, the walls are whitewashed as they will have been for centuries, and the floor is roughly paved. The nave benches are less interesting than the fittings further east: the remains of a rood screen on the north side and a seventeenth-century reading desk on the south side. This previously stood on the south side of the altar opposite an elevated pulpit with tester above on the north side. It is likely that the original rood screen was a two-storey affair, with a loft above. The east window has clearly been enlarged as it cuts into a former niche. All around this window the wall has been painted with texts in Welsh. Above, the heavy oak roof structure would originally have been hidden by boarding, probably also painted. The attractive sanctuary arrangement, with barley-twisting to the altar legs and rails, and a panelled reredos behind, are seventeenth century.

AV

133. LLANGELYNNIN (St Celynnin), Church in Wales   *Gwyn. (M)*

Location: on the A493, 6 miles north of Tywyn.
Access: generally open.

Perched on the coastline and with distant views of Bardsey Island (Ynys Enlli) if the weather is kind, St Celynnin looks more like a barn than a church. It is approached through a lychgate and small cattle grid, then through a south porch which has unusually a bellcote above its gable; but, before entering, notice the way the stonework changes on each elevation, witness to an earlier twelfth-century church that had lower walls and a steeper roof. The structure we see today, with its remarkably wide and shallow roof, is largely fifteenth century.

The interior of the church escaped the hand of the Victorian church restorers and contains a number of fine fittings and fixtures: a low chancel screen that incorporates parts of a medieval rood screen, a painted Commandments board, a horse-bier, simple Shaker-like benches with the names of local inhabitants and farms painted on the back rails, and fragments of wall paintings. Those above the pulpit were discovered during the restoration work carried out by Harold Hughes in 1917, and the memento mori on the west wall was uncovered in 2004 when further repair work was also carried out.

Without electricity and other modern intrusions, one can peacefully sit in the church believing time stopped a century or two ago.

AV

134. LLANGWYLLOG (St Cwyllog), Church in Wales   *Angl.*

Location: by itself off the B5111, 3 miles north-west of Llangefni.
Access: service on the third Sunday of the month at 2 p.m.

This is the earliest and finest of several pre-ecclesiological church interiors in Anglesey, the others being at Llandyfrydog, Llanfaelog, Llanffinan and Talyllyn. The church was refurnished in 1769 with a three-decker pulpit in the middle of the north wall of the nave. There are box pews to the east of the pulpit and open benches to the west. The altar is railed on three sides with seats for communicants along the north and south walls of the chancel. The walls are lined with hat pegs and the parish chest dates from 1804.

NY

135. LLANRHYCHWYN (St Rhychwyn), Church in Wales   *Conwy*

Location: either steep hill from Trefriw direction or via Llyn Geirionydd –
both are spectacular. The church is 2 miles north-west of Llanrwst.
Access: generally open.

St Rhychwyn's is one of those typical Snowdonian churches that you
feel has stood in its remote upland location since time immemorial. It
has twin aisles or, more correctly, a nave and a north aisle; both look very
similar, but the nave is older and each has a different roof construction.
The exterior is plain and simple, just four stone walls and a rugged slate
roof. Inside, very little has changed since the eighteenth century. The
delightfully simple sanctuary has a wooden table surrounded on three
sides in Laudian style by a turned balustrade (1636). Matching this at the
east end of the north aisle is a double-decker pulpit and desk, dated 1691.
There is a choice of no fewer than six bench types to sit on (a particularly
fine one of 1769 on the south wall of the nave). A square stone font
(possibly twelfth century) hides behind the westernmost pier separating
the two aisles, and there is old glass of the fifteenth to seventeenth
centuries in the windows. The walls are whitewashed and the floor paved
in rough slate slabs (beware of slipping when they are wet). Where else
could one find a medieval door held shut by a chain with a twig to secure
it? Access is tricky in wet weather, but when it is fine and dry, the trek is
well worth the effort, both for the church and the superb views of the
Conwy valley.

AV

136. LLANRWST (St Grwst), Church in Wales   *Conwy*

Location: in town centre.
Access: generally open.

Much of Llanrwst church is a rebuild over the original fifteenth-
century one. The continuous nave and chancel retain elements of
the Perpendicular church (central south window, the east window, south
doorway, roof structure) but the tower is early nineteenth century, and

c.1882–4 the church was restored and the north aisle was added by Paley and Austin.

The finest parts of the church are the rood screen (c.1500), very similar to the one in Conwy church, and the Gwydir chapel. This was added by Sir Richard Wynn of Gwydir in 1633–4 and is, in the words of the Pevsner guide, 'a little treasure box of a chapel'. The carved timber panelling around the walls is exquisite and contains some remarkable engraved brass plaques (originally set in the floor). The larger stone coffin with quatrefoils along its sides is reputedly that of Llywelyn the Great. The marble tablet on the east wall, by Nicholas Stone, records the building of the chapel and lists Wynn's 'remarkable Pedigree'.

The setting of the church is lovely and is an intriguing combination of urban and rural. The approach is down a narrow lane with the Jesus Hospital almshouses along one side (c.1610–12), a sexton's cottage on the other, and between them the gateway into the churchyard. Once through this, the river and hills beyond take over, and the bustle of the town feels far behind.

AV

137. MAENTWROG (St Twrog), Church in Wales   Gwyn. (M)

Location: in village at the junction of the A470 and A496, 7 miles east of Porthmadog.
Access: generally open.

A church has possibly stood here since the time of the sixth-century St Twrog, a companion of Beuno. Outside the west end of the church is Maen Twrog, a stone that he hurled in anger from the mountain onto a heathen altar. It bears the marks of his fingers and thumb. The rector here from 1572 until his death in 1623 was Edmund Prys, poet and author of the most singable metrical version of the Psalms in Welsh. A new church was built in 1814, in Churchwarden Gothic, with a bell turret and quatrefoils on the west wall. In 1896 it was miraculously transformed by Douglas and Fordham. They put tracery into the windows, and added a splendid roof supported on timber piers, so creating aisles. They also added the lofty chancel, and the tower with its shingled low-broached spire, whose quirky outline is typical of Douglas. Above the nave arcades the plaster panels are decorated with pretty stencilling; in the chancel there are angels. The benefactors were Mr and Mrs W. E. Oakeley, of Plas Tan-y-Bwlch (enlarged for them by Douglas in 1872). An inscription tablet – in the style of Richard Wynne, but more sophisticated – records that Mrs Oakeley did 'all the carving' in the church. The porch and lychgate (1897) are half timbered, the latter infilled with stone slabs. It is a pity that the church was last re-slated in thin blue slates, instead of the previous rougher brownish ones.

PH

138. NANHORON (Capel Newydd), Independent   *Gwyn. (C)*

Location: take A4413 from Mynytho towards Botwnnog and turn left before reaching Bodlondeb (last farm on the left before reaching Z-bend), drive down bumpy track and turn left at fork near Tŷ Bricks; look for slate sign at gateway on right. Very muddy track from gate to chapel, so take gumboots. Access is not possible from the lane west of the chapel. *Access*: key available from Bodlondeb (telephone: 01758 730277).

There can be very few churches or chapels remaining in Wales that have been as little changed or modernised as Capel Newydd. The chapel sits on its own in the fields, with sheep and cows grazing up to its front door. Indeed, the chapel may have started life as a barn, but was converted to use as an Independent chapel around 1770, the first Nonconformist one in Llŷn outside Pwllheli, the nearest town.

The exterior is as unremarkable as any fieldstone barn in its simplicity, but the interior is extraordinary, and crossing the threshold is a step back in time. Down both sides are box pews and, at the far end, tiered seating probably for children or servants. Midway along the south side is the raised pulpit, reputedly from a disused local church; down the middle the floor comprises compacted earth and is green with moss. The walls are whitewashed and flaking. Above the west door is a timber bier. Outside, to south and east are simple slate gravestones.

AV

139. PENMON (St Seiriol), Church in Wales   *Angl.*

Location: 4 miles north-east of Beaumaris on the lane to Penmon Point.
Access: generally open.

If there is one key site on Anglesey, it must be Penmon. Here can be seen a steady development of Christian art from the tenth to the thirteenth centuries and, indeed, beyond if the collection of buildings is considered as a whole.

St Seiriol's may have been founded in the sixth century by Cynlas, who then put his brother Seiriol in charge. It was a *clas* church of some importance, with links to a sister foundation on nearby Ynys Seiriol (Puffin Island) before becoming an Augustinian priory church. The conventual buildings lay to the south: a cloister immediately south of the chancel (discovered below the present garden in 1923) and a refectory and dormitory block beyond. Both establishments were dissolved in 1538.

The nave is the earliest part, perhaps 1140, and the tower and transepts a few decades later (but the present north transept and east wall of the south transept are Victorian rebuilds). The chancel we see now is also mostly Victorian (1855, by Weightman and Hadfield of Sheffield) but it lies above a fifteenth-century rebuild of a smaller thirteenth-century chancel. The roofs are also renewed. Despite these later developments, St Seiriol's remains the most complete twelfth-century building on Anglesey.

The interior of the church is important for its architectural features and a number of stone monuments now displayed. There is little to detain one in the chancel, which is disappointing in relation to the rest. But go up the steps into the crossing, and there the full force of Romanesque architecture is apparent, for example, the chevron and chequer pattern decoration carved on the south and west archways. Inside the south transept on the south and west walls is some fine arcading, and reset above the west side one of the very few sheila-na-gigs in Wales and the bearded figure of a mason (was he the mason of St Seiriol's?). There are more carved heads above the arch in the nave but, before leaving the south transept, notice the fragments of medieval glass reset in the 1855 window: St Christopher, not entirely inappropriately given the narrow channel of water between Penmon Point and Ynys Seiriol. In the south transept and the nave, there are two carved crosses (c.1000) of great importance. Neither originates in the church but both show foreign influence in the carved patterns. The ring-chain pattern on the back of the nave cross is characteristic of a school of carving also on the Isle of Man. The font is similarly carved and may originally have been a cross base. Outside the south door of the nave, the semicircular tympanum displays more decorative interlace but set within it is a beast biting its own tail, again showing influence from beyond Wales.

AV

140. PENMYNYDD (St Gredifael), Church in Wales　　　　Angl.

Location: leave Menai Bridge on the B5420 towards Llangefni and turn right just before reaching Penmynydd; the church is about a mile along the lane, on the right.
Access: notice regarding key holder in church porch.

St Gredifael's is a little-altered church of the late fourteenth century that replaced an earlier structure of which there are no remains except for some pieces of chevron-decorated stone reused externally in the chancel walls. The porch and north chapel extension were added in the fifteenth century. It has a lofty and spacious interior.

Like so many others, the church underwent restoration in the mid-nineteenth century by the diocesan surveyor, Henry Kennedy. However, the restraining hand of the Revd Henry Longueville Jones, pioneer conservationist and first secretary of the Cambrian Archaeological Association, prevented Kennedy from carrying out a more drastic restoration, and so the windows we see today, for example, are still the originals. Victorian pews can be dull, but here they are particularly splendid and each pew end is adorned with a poppy head. The reredos, the altar rails, the pulpit and the timber partitions around the pair of vestries at the back complete this fine ensemble, all inspired by medieval fittings.

The chief attraction must be the alabaster tomb now in the chapel, once in the chancel. Most sources indicate a date of c.1385, but it is more likely to date from a hundred or so years later than this, and was executed in memory of Gronw Fychan, or Goronwy ap Tudur, and his wife Myfanwy. Goronwy was forester of Snowdon and companion of the Black Prince, and died from drowning in 1382. He was brother of Maredudd, great-grandfather of Henry VII, hence the Tudor link with Anglesey. Note the arms of Tudor sketched on the shields (and the Tudor rose in the chapel window). The tomb is very similar to one in Beaumaris church, to William Bulkeley and his wife, so perhaps they are both by the same hand and both commissioned by the wealthy Bulkeleys.

AV

141. PISTYLL (St Beuno), Church in Wales   *Gwyn. (C)*

Location: on the B4417, 2 miles north-east of Nefyn.
Access: generally open.

An evocative seaside location adds to the appeal of this charming single-cell church. The church, in an oval churchyard, is a simple rectangle, seemingly rising out of the hillside, with a high bellcote on the west end the only break in the roofline. It is entered from the west end through a plain door flanked by buttresses. The interior has rough-cast walls, vernacular timber-truss roof and pegged pews. The interior is very dark, with a rectangular east window in two lights and a tiny twelfth-century window in the east end of the north wall. The medieval font has rough ring-chain decoration of ultimately Scandinavian origin, found also on several fonts in Anglesey – and more generally in sculpture in the Isle of Man, which had late first-millennium connections with north Wales.

Though of high-medieval date, this very simple church may reflect the shape and feel of much earlier churches and is popular for those seeking to revive early 'Celtic' worship. At Christmas, Easter and Lammas rushes and herbs are strewn on the floor.

JW

142. TOWYN (St Mary), Church in Wales *Conwy*

Location: midway between Abergele and Rhyl on the A549.
Access: generally open during the summer.

The saddleback tower of St Mary's is a noteworthy landmark in the flat holiday land of the Clwyd estuary. Church, vicarage and school are all by G. E. Street, and are his best parochial group after All Saints, Boyne Hill, Maidenhead. They were paid for by Robert Bamford Hesketh of Gwrych Castle (as were the Street church at Llanddulas and school at Abergele). Built in 1872–3, the church has a north aisle. The walls are of grey polygonal masonry, with yellow dressings, and the slate roofs are gaily patterned. The tower stands over a vaulted choir. The original furnishings include the reredos, carved by Thomas Earp, the pulpit, the font and the screens and stalls. The ironwork is by Street's favourite smith, James Leaver. The chancel tiles are by Godwin and the glass in the east window (the Te Deum) by Hardman. The vicarage (now a nursing home), linked to the church by a passage, and the school (now a youth club) are of the same materials as the church.

PH

143. TREMADOG (Peniel Chapel), Independent *Gwyn. (C)*

Location: in village on A487, 1 mile north of Porthmadog.
Access: key at Y Wynllan, next to the chapel. Now in the care of the Welsh Religious Buildings Trust.

Peniel Chapel is a key element in the designed village of Tremadog, developed in 1805–12 by W. A. Madocks as a coaching stop on the proposed London–Dublin route (Porth Dinllaen rather than Holyhead was his intended point of embarkation for Ireland). Other elements are the town hall, the inn, the manufactory, the market place and the church (1806–11). It is a mark of Madocks's foresight and liberal views that a Nonconformist chapel was included at all, and it grieved the bishop of Bangor that so much care and money was lavished on a place of worship for non-Anglicans. But Madocks reassured him by pointing out that whereas the chapel was built on sand, the church was founded on good rock.

Both church and chapel were innovative in their own ways. The former St Mary's Church (made redundant in the 1990s and now converted to offices) was one of the first Gothic revival churches in Wales. Peniel Chapel was one of the earliest to be inspired by classical architecture, in particular by St Paul's Church, Covent Garden (Inigo Jones, 1638). But it would be incorrect to exaggerate the shocking and novel appearance the handsome Tuscan portico would have had in 1810 – although in all likelihood Madocks's original design included the portico, it was in fact added later (1849), by which time the classical idiom would have been much more familiar. And, inside, much of what is visible today dates from later years rather than 1810. The gallery originally sat against the entrance gable wall; around 1880, it was extended along two sides and the seating was renewed then, too. The *sêt-fawr* and pulpit date from 1898, and the ceiling from 1908–10. Candles lit the interior in the original chapel; gas lamps were fitted in 1857 and electricity in 1953.

AV

144. TYWYN (St Cadfan), Church in Wales   *Gwyn. (M)*

Location: in town centre.

Access: open daily, 9 a.m.–5 p.m.

St Cadfan's was originally a *clas* church and, following the monastic pattern, had transepts and a central tower. The nave and aisles we see today date from this twelfth-century period. The plain cylindrical piers to the arcades and the rounded arch heads are typical. The arch-braced roof to the nave is later fourteenth century, and almost modern by comparison is the remainder of the church, designed by John Prichard of Llandaff in 1884. He rebuilt the central tower (the original tower had collapsed in 1692 and was replaced by a tower at the west end), the chancel and the transepts. The porch and lychgate were added in 1908 by Harold Hughes, diocesan architect and co-author with Herbert Luck North of *The Old Churches of Snowdonia*.

Set in niches on the north side of the chancel are two early fourteenth-century effigies. The font is probably of the same period. The most important monument is the inscribed stone standing upright in the north aisle. This dates from somewhere between the seventh and the ninth centuries and is particularly important as it is the earliest known inscription in Welsh, carved in half-uncial script, a style used for manuscripts.

AV

145. YNYSCYNHAEARN (St Cynhaearn), formerly Church in Wales, now in the care of the Friends of Friendless Churches   *Gwyn. (C)*

Location: on A497 from Porthmadog to Criccieth, in centre of Pentrefelin, take gated lane south towards sea and follow for about 1 mile; turning and parking space at lychgate.
Access: key obtainable by telephoning either 01766 522871 or 01766 523192 before your intended visit.

Unpromising from the outside, this small remote church will reward those who make the detour with its wonderful and unspoilt interior. It was built around 1830 on the site of a medieval church, and its liturgical layout is interesting because one can almost feel the transformation from a Georgian interior dominated by the pulpit to the later ecclesiological arrangement favoured by the Victorians, where the chancel grows in size, the altar becomes the focus and an atmosphere of reverence and piety begins to pervade. The three-decker pulpit with its curved staircase is particularly fine, as is the staircase to the west gallery. Benches have the names of local families painted on their backs. The elegant little organ is probably by Flight and Robson, the glass in the east and north windows (1899 and 1906) is probably by James Powell & Sons of Whitefriars and, in the churchyard, graves commemorate Black Jack, a black boy brought to Wales as a slave in about 1742, and Dafydd y Garreg-wen, harpist and composer.

AV

4

Churches and Chapels in South Wales

146. BAGLAN (St Catharine), Church in Wales · · · · · · · · · · · · *Neath PT*

Location: on the east side of the A48 between Aberavon and Neath.
Access: services on Sundays at 9 a.m. and 6 p.m. and on Thursdays at 10.15 a.m.

St Catharine's is the most satisfying Victorian church in south Wales, clear and invigorating in design, exquisitely constructed, and containing a full set of contemporary fittings. Only the site disappoints, crowded in by later housing on all sides.

The church was built at the expense of Griffith Llewellyn of Baglan Hall, wealthy as both landowner and industrialist, in 1875–82. As architect, Llewellyn chose his cousin, John Prichard, who had recently brought his great rebuilding of Llandaff Cathedral to a successful conclusion.

The plan is cruciform, the walls on a strongly sloping base. An octagonal crossing tower closely clasped by quatrefoil pinnacles supports a lofty stone spire. The window tracery is in Decorated style in conventional patterns. The stonework, in extremely narrow courses, enhances the sense of scale and dignity in the building.

Internally, the walls are faced with greenish-white Quarella sandstone ashlar, enlivened by bands of amber Penarth alabaster. The jewel-box effect is enhanced by the font, pulpit and sanctuary arcading, also of stone and alabaster. Even the carved pews are to Prichard's design. The tower arches form a sort of canopy over the chancel, resting on shafts with foliage capitals and corbels carved with the heads and the emblems of the four evangelists – the idea is developed from Cheriton church on the Gower. Stained glass by William Morris's firm completes the ensemble, a crucifixion in the east window, St Cecilia and angels in the south transept, all designed by Burne-Jones.

JN

147. BARRY (Bethel Chapel), Baptist — Vale Glam.

Location: in Harbour Road (A4055) at the crest of the hill, before it descends to the docks and Barry Island.
Access: Sunday services at 10.30 a.m. and 6.30 p.m.

The development of Barry Docks in the 1880s created a new town during the following decade. Around the turn of the century a cluster of chapels and one large church went up, mainly for the benefit of middle-class residents in the roads that were occupying the headland to the west of the town. Bethel Baptist is one of these, built in 1902–3 to the design of the prolific chapel architects, George Morgan & Son of Carmarthen.

The exterior, free Gothic in style, makes good use of the steeply sloping site, with an imposing entrance at the upper end, and Sunday schoolrooms slotted in beneath on the downhill side. But it is the interior that impresses. The galleries on three sides are integrated into the chapel structure; an upper tier of columns standing on the gallery fronts carries arches which support the trefoil-profile roof. The lower columns are Tuscan, the upper Corinthian and both are painted white with blue capitals and arch mouldings. Blue reappears in the plaster ceiling between the roof timbers.

Pulpit, baptistery and organ are also ingeniously interlinked. The pulpit can be moved forward for baptisms, and doors behind it to left and right give access to steps up to the baptismal pool. Above sits the organist, and the organ pipes rise to the highest part of the roof.

JN

148. CARDIFF/CAERDYDD (St John the Baptist), Church in Wales

Cardiff

Location: in St John Street, in the pedestrianised city centre.
Access: generally open.

Though in the heart of the modern city, and a mere quarter of a mile from Cardiff Castle, St John's was built not as a parish church, but as a chapel of ease to St Mary's. Its central position in the town explains why it was built on such a scale and in particular why the tower makes such a powerful statement.

The tower is of three tall stages above a vaulted vestibule which is entered by arches on three sides. The principal west window has five lights, a transom and elaborate tracery, but the windows in the upper two stages are quite small. Diagonal buttresses reach as far as the middle of the third stage. At the top, pierced battlements and fantastically elaborated corner pinnacles break out with unexpected exuberance.

The church itself was much enlarged in the nineteenth century, so the fifteenth-century aisled nave and aisled and clerestoried chancel can be understood only inside. The south arcade of the chancel, lower than the rest, is clearly earlier and looks typical of c.1300. Its retention may explain why the fifteenth-century master mason felt the need to add a clerestory to the chancel, to balance its proportions with those of the nave and tower. The five-bay nave has handsome arcades with typical Perpendicular piers, of four shafts and four hollows with polygonal capitals. The arches are steeply pointed. The tower arch is extremely wide and high, wave moulded, the chancel arch is equally wide and high but detailed like the arcades.

Lower outer aisles were added in 1889–91 by Kempson and Fowler, the strange two-storey concrete-framed vestries in the south outer aisle by George Pace in 1975. The north chapel has sixteenth-century timber screens, with early Renaissance decoration, and was the Herbert family chapel. In it is a good early seventeenth-century monument. But what one may study with particular profit here is the Victorian and later stained glass: heraldic glass of c.1855 in the north chapel; apostles and patriarchs designed by William Morris, Ford Madox Brown and Burne-Jones, 1869, in the north-west window of the north inner aisle; next to this Suffer Little Children window, 1890, of opalescent glass to the design of the architect J. P. Seddon; in the outer north aisle another window of 1890, in the idiosyncratic Germanic style of W. F. Dixon; and, the cool climax, the east window of the chancel, Christ and saints, 1915 by Ninian Comper.

JN

149. CARDIFF/CAERDYDD (St Mary), Church in Wales   *Cardiff*

Location: in Bute Street, south of the city centre.
Access: service on Sundays at 11 a.m.

The chief medieval parish church of Cardiff was St Mary's, west of St Mary Street, but it was destroyed by floods in the seventeenth century. The new St Mary's was built further south, to serve Butetown, which developed alongside the docks, in 1840–5, chiefly at the expense of the second marquess of Bute.

The grand elevation to the road looks like the 'west front', with pyramid-roofed towers and three doorways. Entrance is, however, from the other end, and the street elevation conceals a windowless apse. The basilican interior is vast and bare, with a flat plaster ceiling. The arch hood moulds are supported on hideous heads. Only the west gallery survives: originally there were galleries at the sides and a three-decker pulpit in the apse. The Roman Catholic third marquess of Bute used his influence to get the living for Father Arthur Jones, a disciple of Pusey, and in the 1870s he remodelled the interior (with financial assistance from Bute) to suit High Church ideas, calling in John Dando Sedding. He decorated the apse, adding stone statues of the Apostles by Searle of Exeter; he intended to colour these, but never did. He also put in the fine reredos, with a painting of the Adoration of the Kings by Philip Westlake, in a frame by Arthur Grove. The war memorial is by John Coates Carter. At the west end is the magnificent wrought iron screen, in the style of a Spanish *reja*, designed by Cecil Hare for Sedding's church of St Dyfrig (demolished in 1969).

PH

150. CARDIFF/CAERDYDD (St David's Cathedral), Roman Catholic

Cardiff

Location: in city centre, to east of St David's Centre.
Access: generally open.

The original Roman Catholic diocese covering the southern part of Wales and Herefordshire, established in 1850, was served by a Benedictine bishop until 1920. The first bishop, Thomas Joseph Brown, established his cathedral in the Benedictine monastery of Belmont, near Hereford, in 1859. In 1916 the diocese was renamed Cardiff and this church, designed by Peter Paul Pugin (son of A. W. N.) and built in 1884–7, was made a co-cathedral with Belmont. In 1920, Belmont lost its cathedral status and was made an independent abbey. Severely damaged in the Second World War, it was restored afterwards by F. R. Baker of Newport. The spacious sanctuary incorporates a nineteenth-century episcopal throne formerly in the monastic cathedral at Belmont. The Stations of the Cross were designed by Adam Kossowski.

NY

151. CARDIFF/CAERDYDD (St Nicholas, Greek Orthodox)

Cardiff

Location: in Bute Street, near St Mary's (see above).
Access: during Sunday services: Matins at 10 a.m., Liturgy at 11 a.m.

The Greek Orthodox community in Cardiff developed from Greek sailors and shipowners who settled in Wales towards the end of the nineteenth century when the city was a thriving port. The church in Butetown was built in 1906 on land donated to the community. Constructed of red brick, the building is typical of many Orthodox churches: plain on the outside with no spires or towers, a square building with a central lantern over its domed roof and with an apse at the east end. Recent restoration work to repair the church after water penetration through the roof has resulted in the addition of a stunning fresco of Christ Pantocrator looking down from the central dome, surrounded by saints and prophets at its base. The fresco work flows down the walls with massive images of Christ drawing Adam and Eve up from Hades, and of St Nicholas saving sailors at sea. At the east end of the church the traditional icon screen separates the main body of the church from the sanctuary. The screen displays painted icons of Christ, the Mother of God, angels and saints. The Holy Doors in the centre of the screen lead into the sanctuary, as do two side doors. These doors are generally closed and curtained except during services. Without entering the sanctuary, visitors should look through to see the altar table, symbolising the throne of God in heaven, and the windows filled with stained glass images of Orthodox saints.

AA

152. CARDIFF/CAERDYDD (Ebeneser Chapel), Independent

Cardiff

Location: at the north end of Charles Street, accessible from the pedestrianised Queen Street to the north.

Access: the chapel is open for various weekday events, and for Sunday services at 10.30 a.m. and 6 p.m.

Ebeneser is one of the most active of Cardiff's city-centre chapels, the present congregation having moved here in 1976 from Paradise Place. The chapel was built in 1854–5 by an architect, R. G. Thomas of Newport, who later emigrated and built up a successful career in Australia. The building itself has something cosmopolitan about it, as the pepper-and-salt crazy-paving walls are largely faced with stone brought into Cardiff as ballast in returning coal ships. The style of the building was, for its day, adventurous, for it is full-blown Gothic, in a well-understood Decorated idiom. In the 1850s Gothic was hardly yet being used for chapels, and Thomas's building would happily pass as an Anglican church, but for the basement Sunday school.

Inside, the open timber roof and the gallery confined to the west end look church-like too; the single cast-iron column with vine-leaf capital supporting the gallery is splendidly substantial. The stained glass is unusual, too, although only the glass in the big window over the entrance dates back to the 1850s. The pulpit of 1987 and organ of 1999 recessed behind are both in a bold modern style.

JN

153. CARDIFF/CAERDYDD (Tabernacl Chapel), Welsh Baptist

Cardiff

Location: in the Hayes, near the south end of the pedestrianised centre of Cardiff.

Access: open on Saturdays, 9 a.m.–12.30 p.m.

Standing in the centre of Cardiff, in a broad pedestrianised street, set back handsomely behind a railed forecourt, and with a capacity of almost 1,000, Tabernacl has played host to several Welsh national services: in 2000 the Millennium Service attended by the prince of Wales was held here, while the equivalent service for England and Scotland took place in St Paul's Cathedral and St Giles Cathedral, Edinburgh, respectively.

The chapel was built in 1865 to the design of John Hartland, a talented local architect who died young. Although without a portico and rendered and painted to look like ashlar stone, the façade is a fine, coherent classical composition. The centre with four entrance doorways below and four arched windows above, is treated as a channelled basement and richly modelled *piano nobile*. Turret-like staircase bays close the composition.

The interior is largely unaltered, filled with light and colour. Galleries surround it on all four sides. The ground-level pews are grained a mustard colour, the *sêt-fawr* and pulpit are of polished wood and the gallery fronts are decorated with pierced cast-iron panels painted white. The organ, supplied by Griffin & Stroud of Bath, dates to 1907. But what stays most vividly in the memory is the stained glass in the windows on all four sides. On three, there are the names of virtues framed in sky-blue drapery, and above the entrance two scenes are treated pictorially, the Baptism of Christ in the river Jordan and the Last Supper. They all commemorate a famous pastor, the Revd Charles Davies, who died in 1927.

JN

154. COITY (St Mary), Church in Wales   *Bridg.*

Location: in village centre on the northern outskirts of Bridgend.
Access: Sunday service at 9.30 a.m.

Beside the extravagantly ruined remains of Coity Castle stands the complete and hardly altered church of St Mary. The church must have been built early in the fourteenth century for the benefit of the lord of the castle, one of the Turbervilles. Its principal entrance is at the west end, closest to the castle, with the largest, most handsome window above it. The plan is cruciform, a high, wide nave (with small south porch), square crossing between short transepts, and long, quite low chancel. This, and the use of broad chamfers rather than mouldings to emphasise openings, are reminiscent of St Crallo, Coychurch, nearby – the same team of masons may have built both. Coity, however, is the later, as is shown by the full-blown Decorated patterns of the window tracery, more advanced than at Coychurch.

To appreciate the design of the church and its ceremonial arrangements one should start at the west end and move eastwards. The west and south doorways, the one for the lord and his family, the other for parishioners, both have holy water stoups. The spacious nave is visually linked to the transepts by two wide squints, which would have allowed the congregation to see Mass being celebrated at altars in the transepts. These altars each have an ogee-headed piscina, and a narrow diagonal squint, so that the celebrants in the transepts could synchronise the most significant moments of the Mass with the celebration at the high altar in the chancel. The greater ceremonial in the chancel is indicated in the usual way, by an enriched piscina and sedilia.

One movable medieval fitting survives, a wooden Easter Sepulchre, carved with symbols of Christ's Passion – a great rarity. Now in the south transept, it would in the Middle Ages have been placed on the north side of the high altar during Holy Week. Otherwise, there are only two loose and curiously small fourteenth-century effigies. The interior is attractively light and airy, the walls cream washed, the windows clear except for the stained glass above the altar (1863) by William Morris's firm.

JN

155. COWBRIDGE/Y BONTFAEN (United Free Church),

Independent   *Vale Glam.*

Location: standing back on the north side of Westgate, near the west end of Cowbridge's main street.

Access: open on Wednesday, Thursday and Saturday mornings for refreshments.

Ramoth chapel was built in 1828 for a Baptist congregation formed in 1820. In 1971 the Baptists in Cowbridge formally merged with The Limes Presbyterian church to form the present congregation. The chapel and its environs, however, remain much as they were in 1828.

The chapel is a white rendered box under a pyramidal slate roof. The façade is simple, with three round-headed windows, the central one short over the round-headed doorway, the side ones long, to light both vestibule and gallery.

Internally, the same simplicity and lack of artifice prevail. There are simple buff-painted pews and, in the galleries, raked seating. The pulpit platform is dignified by a bowed balustrade all across. The stone baptismal pool is beneath the floorboards in front of the pulpit. Unfortunately, the plaster ceiling has been renewed in fibreboard and from it hang harsh modern lights.

JN

156. COYCHURCH/LLANGRALLO (St Crallo), Church in Wales

Bridg.

Location: in village centre on the southern outskirts of Bridgend.

Access: Sunday service at 9.30 a.m.

The long, aisled nave of *c.*1300 belongs to a cruciform plan, with a plain crossing tower rebuilt after a collapse in 1877. The main features externally are the west front composition and the long chancel. The west doorway is emphasised by mouldings on the arch and by side shafts with shaft-rings. Above are three lancets within a deeply chamfered arch. Buttresses separate the nave from the lean-to aisles, with their unusual pointed quatrefoil west windows. The chancel has closely spaced side lancets and an east window with intersecting tracery, later in style than the rest.

Inside, the nave, in spite of its aisles, feels high and narrow, under a fifteenth-century wagon roof. The ceilure over the east bay shows where the rood stood, high on its loft. Beyond the tower arches opens the lovely, light-filled chancel, its side walls zigzagging compositions of window splays under continuous undulating hood moulds. On the south side the three gabled sedilia and piscina carry on the theme.

The most important objects within the church are the Late Saxon crosses at the west end of the aisles, brought in from their original positions in the churchyard. Overall interlace decoration, a (worn) inscription and the completeness of the northern one make these among the finest Saxon crosses in south Wales.

JN

157. EWENNY (Priory Church of St Michael), Church in Wales

Vale Glam.

Location: three-quarters of a mile down a lane running north-east from the village centre on the B4524, 2 miles south of Bridgend.
Access: both parts of the church are open during daylight hours.

Ewenny Priory is one of the most romantic ecclesiastical sites in south Wales, the church Early Norman at its most powerful. William de Londres (d.1126) built a church at Ewenny and gave it to St Peter's Abbey, Gloucester. His son, Maurice, confirmed the gift in 1141 and founded the monastic community. The present church was probably built by Maurice, in what was by the 1140s a rather old-fashioned style.

The church has the usual cruciform plan, with paired chapels opening from the transepts. It survives intact, except for the north transept and its chapels. Today the parishioners of Ewenny worship in the nave, just as they may have done in the Middle Ages. Its north arcade is a wonderfully robust piece of Early Norman architecture with its stout round piers and round-headed windows in the expanse of wall above. The south wall is solid, with windows only high up, because the monks' cloister abutted against it. To the east, behind the modern altar, the medieval pulpitum wall separates the

16. Ewenny, medieval Priory Church of St Michael. *Jonathan Wooding*

nave from the monastic part of the church; in 2006 the separation was made complete by a glass wall filling the arch above, engraved with a large cross and a cloud of butterflies: an unconventional representation of the Resurrection (by Alexander Beleschenko of Swansea).

The visitor can enter the crossing and choir through a door on the north side. This part has a museum-like atmosphere, full of monuments and fragments of cut stone. These have been consolidated, and in the crossing and transept a new stone floor laid, in 2001–6 (architect Peter Bird of Caröe & Partners). Here, too, the Early Norman architecture is remarkable, the eastern arm tunnel-vaulted with transverse ribs, and wide and high crossing arches on curiously short, paired colonnettes. The early fourteenth-century pierced timber screen is also a great rarity.

The objects on display in the crossing and transept all belong to the church or its Saxon predecessor. There are fragments of Late Saxon cross-shafts and headstones, found reused in the walls of the present church, and monuments to members of the various families that owned Ewenny over the centuries. The most beautiful without a doubt is the early thirteenth-century grave slab of the priory's founder, Maurice de Londres. It is perfectly preserved, with elaborate carved foliage and a handsome incised French inscription. Another piece of exquisite carving dates from five centuries later, the draped oval wall monument to Richard Carne, who died in 1713.

JN

158. LLANCARFAN (St Cadoc), Church in Wales   Vale Glam.

Location: in village west of the A4226 from Bonvilston to Barry and 2 miles north of Cardiff Airport.
Access: key available from either of the two houses south of the churchyard.

The church, in a large grassy churchyard, and several substantial houses cluster in a wooded hollow. St Cadoc was one of the founders of Christianity in south Wales in the sixth century, and is thought to have established an important monastic community here.

The medieval stone south porch, provided with external scratch dial and internal holy-water stoup, opens through a reset thirteenth-century doorway into a wide fourteenth-century aisle that extends the full length of the church with large windows, their tracery of the simplest style. The nave arcade is thirteenth-century again, plain pointed arches on plain square piers with endearingly rustic corbel capitals carved with heads or bunches of grapes. The earliest evidence is in the Norman stonework of the tower arch and chancel arch, though both were subsequently widened and given pointed arches. The roofs, of late medieval wagon form throughout, unify the internal spaces.

The large north window in the chancel, five-light, square headed and with very fanciful tracery, is hard to explain. The tomb recess nearby is too small to have belonged with it. Did it illuminate the site for a portable Easter Sepulchre, like the one at Coity? The rich, if mutilated, canopy work of the reredos shows that St Cadoc's did possess exceptional timber fittings. The screen enclosing the Raglan chapel in the east bays of the south aisle is not exceptional, but the church must once have had a magnificent rood loft across its full width. Post-Reformation traces are the painted Creed on the south aisle wall and a few small monuments, especially the naive little tablets of 1620 and 1666 in the chancel.

JN

159. LLANDAFF (Cathedral Church of St Peter and St Paul, St Teilo, St Dyfrig and St Euddogwy), Church in Wales *Cardiff*

Location: in the north-western suburbs of Cardiff, reached from the city centre up Cathedral Road, A4119, or from the M4, junction 32, along the A4054. *Access:* generally open.

The Norman cathedral was begun by Bishop Urban in 1120; its chancel arch survives to demonstrate the much grander scale of the new building. A second rebuilding at the beginning of the thirteenth century, in an early Gothic style, greatly extended the cathedral westwards and added a square chapter house on the south side. The present west front, nave and choir all belong to this phase. Around 1300 the building was extended eastwards, with a new presbytery copying the early thirteenth-century parts, and a new Lady chapel. The aisles were updated *c.*1330 with new two-light windows. The west front seems always to have had towers, but the north-west tower was rebuilt *c.*1490.

After the Reformation two centuries of disgraceful neglect ensued: the principal roofs fell in and the south-west tower fell down. In 1734, the architect John Wood of Bath undertook to roof over the choir to form a worship space, and this classical oddity remained in use for a century. From the 1840s the cathedral's fortunes revived, as a great restoration programme got under way, promoted by Dean Conybeare and realised by the Pugin-inspired genius of the local architect, John Prichard. In place of Wood's 'temple' the thirteenth-century structure was restored and given a new high-gabled roof. Prichard created a spectacular west front by recreating a showy Somerset-style crown for the north-west tower and constructing an entirely new south-west tower in an early thirteenth-century French Gothic style, with a lofty spire. Prichard's partner, J. P. Seddon, arranged for his Pre-Raphaelite friends to supply gorgeous new fittings and stained glass.

The landmine which exploded in 1941 outside the south aisle inflicted grievous damage. Again the building had to be re-roofed. But again the dean, Glyn Simon, and the architect, George Pace of York, rose to the challenge. This time the style of the day was embraced, no longer revived Gothic, but the uncompromising ideas of Le Corbusier and the expressionism of Epstein and John Piper.

Dominating the nave is Epstein's hieratic figure of Christ, which seems to hover in front of the cylindrical organ case on a pair of giant concrete parabolic arches. All this is Pace's conception, the arches marking the division between nave and choir. Beyond are his intricately canopied choir stalls. Above and beyond are the singing colours of Piper's and Reyntiens's Supper at Emmaus window.

On the north side of the nave are two side chapels which must not be missed. In the chapel under the north-west tower is Dante Gabriel Rossetti's Pre-Raphaelite altarpiece *The Seed of David*, painted in 1855–64 for the high altar. A little way along the north aisle and entered through a richly carved Late Norman doorway is George Pace's other major contribution, St David's Chapel (Welch Regimental Chapel). Inside the entrance is a shattered medieval figure of Christ, beyond which the chapel, with its smooth plastered apse and vault and its tiers of incised inscriptions, encourages tranquil reflection.

The eastern Lady chapel has windows filled with Comper-style glass by Geoffrey Webb, its late medieval reredos enlivened by gilt-bronze posies by Frank Roper of Penarth (1964).

JN

160. LLANFRYNACH (St Brynach), Church in Wales   *Vale Glam.*

Location: best approached on foot from the crossroads on the B4270, 1 mile south-west of Cowbridge.
Access: key available from the Cross Inn, 200 yards south.

This rugged little building has largely escaped Victorian improvement. The west tower is typical of Vale churches, with semi-fortified top, the nave has only one sizeable window, west of the south porch, and the blocked east window in the chancel has never been unblocked (traces of wall paintings beside it). Datable features are mostly late medieval; but the plain, pointed tower arch and chancel arch may indicate a thirteenth-century origin. There is evidence of the rood-loft arrangements in the stair projection in the north wall and the squint high above the chancel arch, to allow someone in the loft to see the priest celebrating Mass in the chancel.

The pews are early twentieth century and unforgettable with their ballooning ends. Various memorials have been arranged left and right of the chancel arch. The one to examine is to Reynold Deere (d.1815), a typical Regency piece with a relief of his two grieving daughters. Henry Wood of Bristol signs it.

JN

161. LLANTWIT MAJOR/LLANILLTUD FAWR (St Illtyd), Church in Wales *Vale Glam.*

Location: on the western edge of Llantwit Major.
Access: generally open.

The large and complicated church of St Illtyd stands at the head of a little valley running towards the Bristol Channel. The first sight from the east is of a plain square tower rising out of a medley of slated roofs. To get a better understanding one should go round to the south, where the entrance is heralded by the churchyard cross up six high steps (carved head replaced 1919) and by the two-storey south porch. Beyond, to the west, is a roofless part, built as a two-storey chantry chapel and abandoned at the Reformation.

Inside, the history of the building unfolds in all its extent and complexity. The porch opens into the 'western church', and here at the west end stand three large and splendid Celtic crosses, datable to the ninth and early tenth centuries, which belonged to the Celtic monastery and school traditionally founded by Illtyd before 600.

The fabric of the church, however, is all much later, from the twelfth to the fifteenth centuries, when Llantwit Major belonged to Tewkesbury Abbey, Gloucestershire, and served as one of their monastic granges or farms.

The 'western church' is in origin Norman as the form of the south doorway suggests, but was almost all rebuilt later; the porch is fourteenth century, the beautiful open timber roof typical of c.1500 in these parts. The tower, immediately to the east, must, with its four arches, have been built as a crossing tower, though no trace of transepts remains. The tower arch pier capitals were originally carved with scallops and stylised foliage typical of the transition from Norman to Gothic around 1200 – and further loose fragments from these capitals are displayed nearby, exquisite carvings worth close examination. The Jesse-tree niche set in the south pier of the chancel arch must belong to the same period, and may originally have served as a reredos behind the high altar of the Norman church. The figure of Jesse lies on a panel at the bottom, and the

17. 'Samson' monument and early medieval carved crosses, Llantwit Major, St Illtyd.
Jonathan Wooding

twining branches that grow from his body and enclose the heads of his descendants (and Christ's ancestors) surround a trefoil-headed niche, in which there must originally have stood a statue of Christ.

So now we are in the main body of the church, an aisled nave and chancel. The architecture is massive and extremely plain, the pointed arcade arches suggesting a thirteenth-century date. On the whitewashed wall surfaces are several large and well-preserved medieval paintings, a St Christopher over the north arcade and above the chancel arch a large patterned area which must have been a decorative background for the rood figures of the crucified Christ, Mary and John. Since 1959, when Alan Durst's rood was set up in front of it, the painting has served this purpose again. On the north wall of the chancel is the figure of St Mary Magdalene, identifiable by the cup of ointment which she holds.

The climax of the medieval interior is the richly carved stone reredos which extends full width in front of the east wall. The elaborate arrangement of ogee-headed and pinnacled niches in two rows must have held statues, destroyed at the Reformation. Doorways at the outer ends gave access to the space behind the altar. To the south is a fine contemporary piscina. The reredos is datable to the second quarter of the fourteenth century and the character of the moulding links it to contemporary work at Wells Cathedral.

JN

162. MAESTEG (Bethania Chapel), formerly Welsh Baptist, now in the care of the Welsh Religious Buildings Trust *Bridg.*

Location: on the west side of the A4063, close to the railway station.
Access: key available from Cyril Phillips, telephone: 07870 423086.

Bethania was built in 1908, by the leading chapel architect of the day and native of Maesteg, William Beddoe Rees. Rees believed that chapels should be classical, as opposed to the Gothic normal for churches of the Establishment. It retains its galleried and vaulted interior, emulating Wren's St James Piccadilly, and its array of craftsmanly fittings, pews laid out on a gently curving plan and *sêt-fawr*, pulpit rostrum and organ all in an integrated design.

JN

163. **MARGAM** (St Mary), Church in Wales *Neath PT*

Location: up a lane leading off the A48 immediately south-east of the roundabout at junction 34 of the M4.
Access: open daily, 10.30 a.m.–4 p.m.

The historical importance of St Mary's church is very great, as it consists of the six westernmost nave bays of the Cistercian abbey founded in 1147 by Robert, earl of Gloucester and lord of Glamorgan. Nowhere else in Britain has so much of a mid-twelfth-century Cistercian church survived to demonstrate the blunt austerity of Cistercian architecture during the first wave of expansion by the order.

The west front, of grey Sutton stone ashlar, does have some decoration on the central entrance doorway and three upper windows, in their arch mouldings and shafts with many plump shaft rings. It is the interior that represents the Cistercian ideal. Big, high, cruciform piers carry the plainest of imposts and unmoulded semicircular arches which continue the lines of the piers. In the sheer walls above are traces of small blocked clerestory windows. The aisles, with plain plastered groin vaults, were all reconstructed in 1805–9 and 1872–3.

The second restoration, promoted by Theodore Talbot of Margam Castle, was intended to make the church a setting for ritualistic worship, and later fittings and stained glass have enhanced this character, especially the mighty brass sanctuary lamps and the smouldering glass of 1905 by Powell's in the east window.

After the Dissolution the abbey and its lands came into the hands of Sir Rice Mansel of Oxwich. At the east ends of the aisles the Mansels and their heirs the Talbots erected one of the best collections of family monuments in Wales. The most ambitious Mansel monuments (south aisle) are early seventeenth century, all of London workmanship with recumbent effigies on decorative tomb chests and obelisks at the angles. The outstanding Talbot monument (north aisle, now vestry) commemorates Theodore, the restorer of the church. Under a gabled and pinnacled canopy lies the hyperrealistic white marble effigy of a devout young man. It is a major work by the sculptor H. H. Armstead and is dated 1881.

JN

164. MERTHYR MAWR (St Teilo), Church in Wales   *Bridg.*

Location: 2 miles south-west of Bridgend, reached from the A48 down a minor road.
Access: generally open.

The church, built in 1849–50, is important as the earliest in Glamorgan to show the new enthusiasm, inspired by A. W. N. Pugin, to recapture a spirit of pure medievalism in ecclesiastical buildings. The architects were the London-based Benjamin Ferrey, a Pugin disciple and his future biographer, and John Prichard of Llandaff, here at the beginning of his career.

The church stands back behind the graveyard on a grassy platform, a model of clarity. The four-bay nave, with gabled south porch and lower two-bay chancel are of grey local limestone, the bays firmly defined by Bath stone buttresses and pilaster strips with a long lancet window in each bay. The roofs are steeply pitched. Overhanging the west gable is an elegant bellcote, its complex design a contrast to the simplicity of the rest.

The interior is a little more elaborate, with shafts framing the three lancets above the altar and supporting the principal roof timbers. The stained glass depicting the Resurrection in the east window was inserted c.1855 and is by Frederick Preedy. The font (its bowl late medieval) is raised on an elaborate arrangement of steps, and the richly shafted pulpit looks like a Prichard design, but must have been made for another building. The Minton floor tiles provide unity throughout.

JN

165. MERTHYR TYDFIL (Zoar Ynysgau Chapel), formerly Welsh Congregational, now in use as a theatre.   *Merthyr*

Location: in town centre, lying back from the west side of Pontmorlais.
Access: during theatrical performances.

Ynysgau Chapel (Zoar was added to the name when congregations merged) demonstrates particularly vividly the early development of Dissenting places of worship in south Wales towns. First built in 1749, it lies back down an alley, barely visible from the main street. The present chapel bears tablets recording repairs in 1821 and a rebuilding in 1825. In 1841–2 the minister, the Revd Benjamin Owen, had it rebuilt again to a design of his own contriving. Such repeated reconstructions reflect the explosive growth of Merthyr Tydfil as the burgeoning ironworks required ever more immigrant workers. Mr Owen's chapel, however, was on an unprecedented scale, seating around a thousand; although it underwent a thorough refitting in the late nineteenth century, no further enlargement was required. Architecturally, the exterior, as one would expect in such a hidden location, is plain, a two-storeyed under a big pyramidal roof. Also in response to the tight site, the entrance is recessed, within a paved lobby behind a pair of roughly shaped stone columns. The dramatic seven-sided gallery which runs almost around the interior, its seating steeply raked, seems to be of the original build of 1842 with contemporary iron-framed windows lighting it on three sides, but the *sêt-fawr*, pulpit and decorated plaster ceiling must all be late nineteenth century.

JN

166. MOUNTAIN ASH (Bethania Chapel), Welsh Congregational

Rhondda

Location: on the corner of Philip Street, behind the Town Hall, on the north-east side of the River Cynon.
Access: service on Sundays at 3 p.m.

The chapel stands in the tight grid of streets which marks the earliest development of Mountain Ash, a centre of steam-coal mining, in the 1840s and 1850s. In the big full-width pediment is the bold date 1859. The exterior is rendered grey, the façade, behind a tiny railed forecourt, a standard three-bay composition, with square-headed windows below, round-headed above, all enlivened by rusticated surrounds.

The interior by contrast is bright and colourful, unchanged from its Victorian layout and lovingly tended. The pews are grained, with a *sêt-fawr* facing the raised and arcaded pulpit. This stands below a big arch above which runs the exhortation (in Welsh) 'Let every living creature praise the Lord'. Galleries with raked seating extend along the other three sides of the chapel, with a platform for musicians over the entrance. The ensemble is crowned by a joyously coloured ceiling, white with five plaster roundels picked out in brick red. It must date from 1887, when the roof was raised to provide more room for the galleries.

The Sunday school on the downhill side of the chapel also keeps original fittings, raked seats with backs which when tipped forward turn into tables.

JN

167. NEATH (St David), Church in Wales   *Neath PT*

Location: in town centre, facing Victorian Gardens.
Access: open on Friday and Saturday mornings.

This imposing mid-Victorian church, built in 1864–6, is Neath's focal building, dominating the heart of the town and with a steeple visible far and wide. Its construction was promoted by the Revd John Griffiths, rector 1855–96, whose popularity seems to have made fund-raising easy. The architect, John Norton, of Bristol and London, rose to the challenge with zest. The church combines the requirements of Griffiths for a preaching space of large capacity and Norton's enthusiasm for fashionable continental models and constructional polychromy.

The exterior has an Early French Gothic feel in its big plate-traceried clerestory windows, and a soaring tower crowned by a cluster of pyramid roofs, a motif newly popularised by G. E. Street's London church of St James-the-Less. The walls are sombre, of dark brown Pennant sandstone on a grey-green basement, but the Bath stone dressings show up pale and bright after recent cleaning. On the south porch is a large relief carving of St David, with crozier and harp, but the ceremonial west doorway introduces red as well as buff stonework.

The interior consists of a wide nave, with arcades on piers with richly carved capitals, vividly polychrome walls of red and black brick and buff stone (as popularised by Butterfield and Street) and an apsidal chancel ringed with tall close-set traceried windows, another continental effect. The most significant fitting is the lavish marble and alabaster pulpit.

JN

168. NEWTON NOTTAGE (St John the Baptist), Church in Wales

Bridg.

Location: in village centre, approached from A4106, just over a mile east of Porthcawl.

Access: services on Sundays at 8.30 a.m., 11a.m. and 6 p.m. and on Tuesdays and Fridays at 10.30 a.m.

Although the outskirts of Porthcawl have crept round on all sides, the setting of the church remains unspoilt. High walls of local limestone confine the lanes and enclose the churchyard with its packed memorials. The church itself was all built in the early sixteenth century. The walls are of local limestone, but the cut stonework, of greenish-brown sandstone, is unusually elaborate. Thus the west doorway is the centrepiece of a composition with shield-bearing angels and the priest's door on the south side of the chancel has half-length angels carrying its hood-mould. The stoup in the south porch, however, with stiff-leaf foliage, is a reused thirteenth-century piece. The tower top is the common Glamorgan type, with a gabled roof behind corbelled battlements.

The most extraordinary feature of the church is inside: the semicircular stone pulpit corbelled out from the north wall and crudely carved with a scene of the flagellation of Christ. This must be early sixteenth century, too, and may well have been carved by the same masons as the decorative doorways outside. Fragments of contemporary wall paintings have also been recently uncovered: an angel on the south wall of the nave, and a hand holding a sword (from the beheading of St John the Baptist?) on the north wall of the chancel.

JN

169. PENARTH (St Augustine), Church in Wales   *Vale Glam.*

Location: in Church Place South, at the top of the town.
Access: open on the first Wednesday in each month, 2 p.m.–4 p.m., and at service times: Sundays at 8 a.m. and 10.30 a.m.; weekdays (except Tuesdays) at 10 a.m.

There was a medieval church on Penarth Head: its stumpy saddleback tower had for centuries been a landmark for ships entering Cardiff Bay. So when, in 1864, the newly appointed vicar, the Revd Charles Parsons, decided that it should be rebuilt to cater for the town's rapidly expanding population, and Baroness Windsor undertook to pay for the new church, the one condition imposed on the architect, William Butterfield, was that it too should have a landmark, saddleback-roofed tower.

Butterfield was one of the most original church architects of his day, the pioneer in using constructional colour in brick, stone and marble. The church he built at Penarth in 1865–6 is one of the most successful creations of his maturity. The exterior, in an Early Gothic style, is quite austere, faced with local grey limestone. The body of the church is a long, broad, clerestoried nave and a short chancel. There are two entrances reached up long flights of steps on the hillside, one in the north porch towards the docks, the other to the south-west at the base of the tower, for the residents of the newly erected villas in the expanding town.

The strongly coloured interior comes as a shock, lifting the viewer's senses to a higher plane. The structural members, piers, arches and window dressings are of local pink or purple Radyr stone and Bath stone of a strong ochre hue. In contrast, wall surfaces are of red brick, strongly patterned with a lattice design in white and black. The principal fittings, reredos and font are strongly geometrical but subdued in their polychromy. The glass is by Alexander Gibbs, the maker preferred by Butterfield to interpret his ideas.

JN

170. PENTRE (St Peter), Church in Wales   *Rhondda*

Location: beside the A4058 in the centre of Pentre, midway along the Rhondda Fawr.

Access: services on Sundays at 10.30 a.m., Tuesdays at 9.30 a.m. and Thursdays at 6.30 p.m.

Griffith Llewellyn of Baglan Hall invested heavily in the Rhondda as owner of the Tynybedw Colliery and founder at Pentre in 1874 of the Llewellyn and Cubitt engineering works, which became a major supplier of colliery equipment in south Wales. Shortly before his death in 1888, he set aside the generous sum of £20,000 for the construction of a grand church at Pentre. F. R. Kempson, Llandaff diocesan architect, made the design in 1887 and the church opened in 1890. After Llewellyn's death his widow, Madelina Georgina, ensured that every last decorative detail was completed. Since then, the church and its setting have been lovingly maintained, so that they survive virtually unaltered.

The exterior, best seen from the lowest corner of the churchyard in Llewellyn Street, is dominated by the west tower, where the lofty baptistery raises the ringing chamber, clock stage and belfry to the height of 100 feet. Elaborate steps lead up to the main entrance in the south porch. The walls of the church are a sombre brown, but the ashlar dressings are all banded in buff and pink.

This hardly prepares one for the dazzling display of colour inside, the walls striped in buff and pink brick, the stonework in broader bands of the same colours. The long wide nave leads to a raised choir and sanctuary, the latter sheathed in marble and alabaster arcading. On the reredos are carved Christ's Nativity, Crucifixion and Resurrection, and the three large lancet windows above are filled by a depiction of the Ascension, concluding the story. This stained glass is by one of the most flamboyant Late Victorian glass artists, W. F. Dixon, who also executed the St Peter scenes in the tower windows.

JN

171. PETERSTON-SUPER-ELY (Croes-y-Parc Chapel), Baptist

Vale Glam.

Location: on its own half a mile south-west of Peterston-super-Ely village, off the A48, 8 miles west of Cardiff.
Access: service on Sundays at 10.30 a.m.

The chapel was built in 1843, quite late for the 'long-wall' design, where there are two doorways near the outer ends of the façade, with short round-headed windows over and in the centre a pair of long round-headed windows. This arrangement reflects the internal layout, where the pulpit backs on to the centre of the front wall illuminated by the long windows and galleries extend round the other three sides. Here the galleries form five cants, their seating being the usual raked benches. What is surprising is that the original bench seating at ground level also survives. The pulpit, however, must be much later, say c.1900. There is no baptismal pool, as baptisms have always taken place in the nearby river – as they still do.

JN

172. PONTYPRIDD (Tabernacl Chapel), formerly Baptist converted for use as a historical and cultural centre in 1986   *Rhondda*

Location: in Bridge Street, in the town centre.
Access: open Mondays–Saturdays, 10 a.m.–5 p.m.

The chapel was built in 1861, to the design of the minister, Dr E. Roberts, it is said. It is an austere building, of grey rock-faced stone, three bays wide, three deep, and three storeys high, as the galleried chapel stands above a basement Sunday school. What makes Tabernacl memorable is the lavish redecoration it underwent in 1910 at the hands of a local firm of architects, A. O. Evans, Williams & Evans. Conversion for its present use has left much of the 1910 work intact. Here the visitor can feel the surge of optimism that flowed through Welsh Nonconformity in the wake of the Revival of 1905–6. *Sêt-fawr*, pulpit, balustraded organist's bench and, filling the wide arch above, a towering organ, form a rich, unified composition. The rich plaster ceiling is painted with wreaths in warm earth colours, while abstract patterns in sage green and ruby stained glass fill all the windows.

JN

173. PORT TALBOT (St Theodore), Church in Wales   *Neath PT*

Location: on the east side of the A48, midway between Aberavon and Margam.

Access: services on Sundays at 11 a.m. and 6 p.m., Mondays at 7 p.m. and Wednesdays at 10 a.m.

The death of Olive Talbot of Margam in 1894 prompted her sister, Emily, to erect a church in her memory and in that of their brother, Theodore, a devout high churchman who had been killed in a hunting accident back in 1876. The building was intended to provide a capacious place of worship for the expanding town of Port Talbot. John Loughborough Pearson, architect of Truro Cathedral and many other lofty vaulted churches, was commissioned to design it. The church, which was commenced in 1895 and consecrated two years later leaving the design incomplete, suits its memorialising function. Extremely tall, on a cruciform plan, with a long nave terminating towards the road in an unfinished west tower, the building is faced with sombre local Pennant sandstone with buff Bath stone dressings. The windows are not traceried but lancets in groups, the austere arrangement which Pearson preferred.

The interior, unlike those of the other major Victorian churches of Glamorgan, is also largely monochrome. Here the height is even more impressive, the aisled nave three storeyed, and the chancel, south chapel and nave aisles all having the rib vaults which Pearson loved so much. Colour would have been provided by stained glass, but the only glass inserted in Emily Talbot's lifetime is in the south chapel, angels by Clayton and Bell. The large figures of Christ and saints in the lancets above the high altar, of 1983, are disappointingly insipid. The font, in the west baptistery, and the pulpit are the major fittings designed by Pearson.

JN

174. RHYMNEY (Penuel Chapel), Welsh Baptist   *Merthyr*

Location: in Coronation Terrace, in the middle of Rhymney, west of the main street, the B4257.
Access: Sunday service at 6 p.m.

'Penuel Baptist Chapel 1838 rebuilt 1859' reads a tablet on the façade but this is an overstatement, and the building, nearly a square in plan, 55 feet by 52 feet, was erected in 1838–9 and only remodelled twenty years later. The grey-rendered façade, with a big arched central doorway, two short arched inner windows above and two long arched outer windows, has inconspicuous decorative surrounds and angle quoins, all doubtless added in 1859.

The interior, however, is arranged in a way typical of the early nineteenth century, for the pulpit on its rostrum backs on to the vestibule, so that on entering one sees not the pulpit but the imposing five-sided gallery with its steeply raked seating. All is brightly lit by upper windows on all four sides. The galley fronts and the box pews at ground level are all grained yellow-brown and the decoration of the ceiling has recently been picked out in salmon pink.

As in many Baptist chapels, the baptismal arrangements are ingenious. The pool, beneath the rostrum, can be entered from the vestibule through one of the window openings, from which the glazed sash has been temporarily removed.

JN

175. ROATH (St Germain), Church in Wales   *Cardiff*

Location: at the corner of Metal and Star Streets, Splott, an inner eastern suburb of Cardiff south of Newport Road.
Access: the west door is always open and the interior can be viewed through a glass screen; the key is available from either the church hall or the clergy house.

This is the most impressive of Cardiff's Anglo-Catholic churches, designed in 1881–4 by Bodley and Garner. The nave has aisles but no clerestory. The chancel is clerestoried, rising high above the north chapel and the eastern vestry. The exceptionally spacious interior has the elaborate furnishings one would expect of a church in this tradition: the rood, filling the chancel arch, originally designed by Bodley for St Paul's, Lorrimore Square, London; pulpit designed by Cecil Hare; organ case designed by Bodley in 1887; the font, designed by Bodley in 1898, with a later cover by Hare; the reredos, designed by Hare in 1921–2, in the form of triptych of late medieval Dutch type, with gilded statues and shutters added in 1926–7; Stations of the Cross of 1919 by Hare; stained glass by C. E. Kempe and by Burlison and Grylls. The clergy house, designed for a team of unmarried priests, was designed by Bodley and built in 1893–4.

NY

176. ST ATHAN/SAIN TATHAN (St Tathan), Church in Wales
Vale Glam.

Location: St Athan village lies to the north of the B4265, between Barry and Llantwit Major.
Access: generally open.

The cruciform church, crowned by a crossing tower, stands in a stone-walled churchyard in the middle of the village. It is probably of the thirteenth century in origin. What matters is the south transept, which was remodelled in the mid-fourteenth century as a burial chapel for members of the Berkerolles family of East Orchard. Its centrepiece is the magnificent and highly unusual monument erected c.1340 and said to commemorate Sir Roger de Berkerolles, who died in 1351. Recumbent effigies – he in armour holding a heraldic shield, she in fashionable dress, on a tomb chest against which kneel mourners, both monks and laymen – are placed under a large, many-moulded arch. Within the head of the arch is a pointed quatrefoil, below which a bearded figure appears to hover. Flanking canopied niches once held statues, probably of saints. Large Decorated style windows to south, east and west fill the chapel with light. Evidence of the eastern altar, at which a priest would regularly say mass for the souls of Berkerolles and his wife, are the rich piscina in the south-east corner and the diagonal north-east squint, enabling the priest to see the high altar in the chancel. A second monument, with figures of a second Berkerolles knight and lady, is not in its original position. Both monuments have been unwisely tinctured in azure and gold.

JN

177. ST BRIDE'S MAJOR (St Brigid), Church in Wales   *Vale Glam.*

Location: above the village centre, which straddles the B4265, between Bridgend and Llantwit Major.
Access: generally open.

As seen from the east under arching branches, the church looks inviting on the hillside, gabled chancel in front, then the much higher gable of the nave and, crowning the composition, the west tower. The body of the church was heavily Victorianised (1851 by Egbert Moxham), but the tower is a fine late medieval structure, with diagonal buttresses and corbelled battlements with small pinnacles. Notice, too, the churchyard cross, also late medieval, on the north side of the church.

Inside, the tower arch is high and well proportioned, but the low, round-headed chancel arch indicates the Norman origin of the building in the mid-twelfth century. What makes St Bride's Major special is the collection of monuments in the chancel. They illustrate unusually clearly the changing fashions in commemorating the dead over a period of five hundred years.

Earliest is the large stone coffin. Its lid, incised with the figure of a cross-legged knight in chain-mail armour, is at present under the altar, but a rubbing hangs alongside. The shield he holds, and details of the armour identify the figure represented as John le Botiler, who died soon after 1335. The most splendid monument, on the north side of the sanctuary, commemorates John Butler (d.1540) and his wife. Their large effigies lie, excellently lit by a four-light window in the wall behind, on a richly carved tomb chest, against which kneel the small figures of their two sons and two daughters. Above is a large canopy crowned with a rich shield of arms. So this is a dynastic monument of the sort which was as popular before the Reformation as after it.

The hanging monument on the north wall of the chancel to John Wyndham (d.1697) and his wife who died the following year represents a quite different approach. Here it is personal qualities that count. The long inscriptions recount their private and public virtues and above, in a draped recess, are their half-length portraits turned towards each other tenderly, he in a full-bottomed wig and lawyer's cap, she in a widow's veil. Yet, as her veil shows, this is not meant as a realistic conversation piece. Lastly, on the south wall, Sebastian Gahagan's marble wall monument to Thomas Wyndham (d.1814) shows the then fashionable influence of ancient Greek and Roman sculpture, but also emphasises Resurrection. Wyndham is shown on his deathbed, welcomed into heaven by the two young sons who had predeceased him.

JN

178. ST DONATS (St Donat), Church in Wales   *Vale Glam.*

Location: reached along a minor road from Llantwit Major, or from the B4265 at Wick via Monknash and Marcross.
Access: generally open.

The setting of the church is one of the most delightful in south Wales. The building stands in a little valley which runs down to the sea, with hanging woods on one side and on the other the high stone walls of St Donat's Castle. Although parochial it must always have served as virtually a private chapel for the lords of the castle. And, just as the castle was begun in the twelfth century for the de Hawey family, and greatly elaborated in the later Middle Ages for the Stradlings, the same building pattern can be traced in the church.

The chancel arch is established as being of the twelfth century, by its semicircular form and the angle shafted jambs with primitive capitals. Piecemeal rebuilding and enlargement clearly took place from the early fourteenth century onwards. First, the west tower was added, then the north chapel was added to the chancel. The chancel itself was rebuilt in the Perpendicular style a century or so later, and the nave and north porch a little later still. The corbelled parapets with gargoyles to nave and tower closely resemble the late fifteenth-century treatment of the castle hall.

The font is probably twelfth century, if the scale pattern is anything to go by. The remarkable late medieval timber lectern, however, is an importation, as recently as 1913. Several generations of the Stradlings are commemorated by monuments in the church, three by a very rare panel painting dated 1590; Sir Edward (d.1609) by a wall monument with kneeling figures, typical of the period; the last two generations by a white marble armorial tomb chest of c.1738.

In the churchyard is St Donat's particular treasure, a late medieval cross. It stands on three steps, not as many as some, but both the tall shaft and the crosshead have survived, the head carved with the Crucifixion. An even finer cross of similar type survives in the churchyard at Llangan, near Bridgend.

JN

179. ST FAGANS/SAIN FFAGAN (St Mary), Church in Wales

Cardiff

Location: the village lies 1 mile west of the western edge of the Cardiff suburb of Fairwater; the church stands at the south end of the village street, east of the enclosing wall of St Fagans Castle grounds.
Access: services on Sundays at 10.30 a.m. and Wednesdays at 10 a.m.

St Mary's church, though a simple medieval building of chancel, nave with south porch, and west tower, is an excellent place to discover the lively inventiveness of the Decorated style of the early fourteenth century. The windows in the chancel are still Geometrical, having encircled lobed motifs, the hoods of those on the south side resting on heads, human and canine. The south-east window in the nave is in a more advanced style, and must be later, say c.1350. Internally, this window has an extra eastern shaft, carved with a projecting human head, probably a support for the rood beam. The chancel arch, of an elegant steepness, reveals the climax of the church, the rich shafting of the east window and the superb composition of piscina and triple sedilia. The tower is seventeenth century; the north aisle and vestry were added by G. E. Street in 1859–60, at the expense of Baroness Windsor, then owner of St Fagan's Castle. The font is late medieval, the other fittings are Street's. The fine stained glass by Hardman was also inserted by members of the Windsor family, between 1859 and 1874.

JN

180. ST FAGANS/SAIN FFAGAN (Welsh Museum of National History)
Cardiff

Location: in the village of St Fagans on the western outskirts of Cardiff, best approached and signed from the A4232.
Access: open daily, 10 a.m.–5 p.m., admission free.

Two ecclesiastical buildings have been re-erected at the museum. Capel Penrhiw – a Unitarian chapel formerly at Drefach Felindre in the Teifi Valley – dates from 1777. The ground-floor furnishings, with the pulpit in the middle of the long entrance wall, the communion table in front and the box pews on the both sides, are original, but the seating in the gallery, around three sides of the interior, has been reconstructed. The former parish church of Llandeilo Talybont, near Pontarddulais, north-west of Swansea, is a late medieval building completely refurbished in 1810. By the time that it was being dismantled for transportation to the museum the interior had been stripped of its furnishings and an important series of wall paintings revealed. It was, therefore, decided to reconstruct the church as it might have looked in c.1520, on the eve of the Reformation, complete with rood screen and loft, thus providing the United Kingdom with the one genuine representation of what a late medieval church may have looked like. On the walls are modern replicas of the original paintings and there are stone altars in the chancel, at the east end of the south aisle and in the north chapel. Otherwise, the church is empty of furniture. Whilst this is an imaginative piece of reconstruction, the lack of images, candles, or stone seats against the walls for the elderly and infirm to sit on and the beautifully stone-paved instead of earthen floors give a rather cleaned-up version of a replica medieval building.

JN

5

Churches and Chapels in South-East Wales

181. ABERGAVENNY/Y FENNI (St Mary), Church in Wales *Mons*

Location: in town centre.
Access: generally open.

This important former priory church was founded in 1087. Although it was heavily restored and partially rebuilt in a series of restorations between 1881 and 1896, the church preserves many medieval and later furnishings. Chief among these are the handsome twelfth-century font, the magnificent set of fourteenth-century choir stalls, those for the former prior and sub-prior having tall carved canopies and the others with carved and latticed backs, and the remarkable wooden figure of Jesse which formed the back of a medieval reredos. There are also some high-quality modern furnishings. These include the First World War memorial by W. D. Caröe, a crucifixion in the north aisle by Frank Roper (1977) and the south chapel altar by Keith Simpson (1997–8). There is also twentieth-century stained glass by F. C. Eden, John Winbolt and F. W. Cole. The church contains one of the most impressive set of monuments anywhere in the British Isles. In the north transept is the wooden monument to John, Lord Hastings (d.1325). In the south chapel is the tomb of Eva de Braose (d.1257) and the monument to Dr David Lewis, the first principal of Jesus College, Oxford (d.1584). The largest collection of monuments is in the south, or Herbert, chapel. These were restored and rearranged in 1994–8 under the direction of Michael Eastham. They include the tombs of Sir Lawrence and Sir William de Hastings, both of whom died in 1348;

the tomb of Sir William ap Thomas (d.1446) and his wife Gwladys (d.1454); the tomb of Sir Richard Herbert (d.1469) and his wife Margaret; the canopied wall monument to Richard Herbert of Ewyas (d.1510); and the monument to Andrew Powell (d.1631) and William Baker (d.1648), the latter not erected until after the restoration of Charles II in 1660.

NY

182. ABERGAVENNY/Y FENNI (Our Lady and St Michael), Roman Catholic
Mons

Location: in town centre.
Access: generally open.

This unusually grand and elaborate church celebrates the distinguished local Catholic tradition, which kept the faith through penal times. The architect was Benjamin Bucknall, best known for the astonishing unfinished Woodchester Park in Gloucestershire. Built in 1858–60, the church is impressively tall and richly detailed, though much of the carving has never been carried out. The style is Decorated, and the materials local red sandstone with Bath dressings. The east end, facing the road, has a splendid great window. Unfortunately, the tower and spire, intended to go on the south side, were never built. The interior is lofty, and the roofs steep pitched. The reredos was added in 1883, designed by Edmund Kirby of Liverpool and carved by A. B. Wall: the angels are in an orgy of adoration. The glass in the east window is by Hardman. The chapel off the south aisle, added in 1894, commemorates the Baker family and especially Dom Augustine Baker, martyred in 1575. The glass is by Clayton and Bell (1861). There is a painting of St David Lewis (alias Charles Baker), martyred in 1679, and a marble roundel of John Baker Gabb, the solicitor who paid for the church, out of which he fairly pops: it is signed 'Battersby, Roma'. There is also in the church a copy of Raphael's *St Michael* by Kenelm Digby (1861). He was the author of *Mores Catholici* and other books. The church possesses some fine medieval vestments.

PH

183. BETWS NEWYDD (dedication unknown), Church in Wales

Mons

Location: in the village off the B4598, 3 miles north of Usk.
Access: generally open.

A small fifteenth-century church, with a large west porch and double bellcote, lightly restored in 1894. This restoration preserved the contemporary wagon roofs, boarded in the chancel and plastered in the nave, separated by one of the most complete rood-screen arrangements in England and Wales. The screen preserves both the original loft, staircase and doorway, and a tympanum above the loft on which the figures of Christ, Our Lady and St John were probably painted, although they have been obliterated.

NY

184. CHEPSTOW/CAS-GWENT (St Mary), Church in Wales *Mons*

Location: in town centre.
Access: open Mondays–Saturdays, 10 a.m.–4 p.m.

The former priory church was founded before 1075. The building has seen even more alteration than that at Abergavenny, partly as a result of the chancel's having been demolished after the suppression of the priory in 1536 and the collapse of the former central tower, demolishing the transepts, in 1701. In 1838–41 the interior was insensitively remodelled by the addition of a short new chancel and wide transepts, but at the same time the nave aisles were demolished and the arcades blocked up, although the handsome twelfth-century triforium and clerestory was preserved. In 1890, it was decided to restore the church to its medieval plan but the work was eventually abandoned, after the rebuilding of the chancel and south transept, in 1913. Apart from the fifteenth-century font and the handsome monuments to the second earl of Worcester (d.1549) and Margaret Clayton, erected in 1620, the interior furnishings are not outstanding, although the recent replacement of the pews by chairs has created a more spacious interior.

NY

185. CWMYOY/CWM-IAU (St Martin), Church in Wales   *Mons*

Location: by itself on a side road off the A465, 6 miles north of Abergavenny.
Access: generally open.

A delightfully atmospheric twelfth- to fourteenth-century church, its outer walls leaning dramatically as a result of subsidence. It was lightly restored in 1889 and retains its crude medieval roof, twelfth-century font, seventeenth-century communion table and rails and a fine collection of rustic late seventeenth- to early nineteenth-century monuments, including some by the Brute family. The seventeenth-century plaster panels in the porch are an unusual feature.

NY

186. GROSMONT (St Nicholas), Church in Wales   *Mons*

Location: in the village on the B4347, 10 miles north-east of Abergavenny and 12 miles north-west of Monmouth.
Access: generally open.

This large cruciform church, with its octagonal central tower and spire, dates largely from the thirteenth century. The aisled nave and the western aisles to the transepts, all under one sloping roof, are completely unfurnished and have been so since the early nineteenth century, as shown in a contemporary plan of the interior. The eastern part of the church was rather too heavily restored by J. P. Seddon between 1869 and 1879. His are the screen separating this part of the church from the unfurnished nave, the choir stalls and clergy desks, the heavy pulpit of stone and alabaster and the garish reredos under an east window illustrating the Feeding of the Five Thousand. This may have been made by the firm of Heaton, Butler and Bayne and was paid for by J. E. W. Rolls of The Hendre, who had commissioned Seddon's restoration.

NY

187. LLANARTH (St Mary and St Michael), Roman Catholic   *Mons*

Location: in the grounds of Llanarth Court north of the A40, 5 miles south-east of Abergavenny.
Access: Mass on Sundays at 11 a.m.

Llanarth Court, now a hospital, was the home of the Jones family from the seventeenth century until 1947. They kept the Catholic faith, as so many did in Monmouthshire and Herefordshire. At right angles to the house is the church, built in about 1750. It has round-headed windows, and was intended to look like a garden building. The apsidal sanctuary was added *c.*1930, and the west gallery is also later. The most remarkable feature of the interior is the stained glass in five of the windows. The three half-figures of the Saviour and saints and the Circumcision panel are from a Cologne workshop of *c.*1520, while the fifth window has seventeenth-century Swiss or German grisaille glass. The apse windows of *c.*1939 are by Margaret Rope. Outside the apse is a cross with a medieval head: the Crucifixion is on one side and the Virgin and Child on the other.

PH

188. LLANDOGO (St Odoceus), Church in Wales   *Mons*

Location: in village on the A466, 8 miles north of Chepstow.
Access: generally open.

Up the Wye Valley beyond Tintern stands this fancy little church, rebuilt in 1859–61 by J. P. Seddon. Of red sandstone with Bath dressings, inside and out, it is in Geometrical Decorated style. The west porch has a roof of stone slabs on stone ribs. Above, a buttress rises between the pair of windows, supporting a group of shafts which in turn support the perky hexagonal bell turret, which has open arches and a stone spirelet above. In 1889, Seddon and his partner, John Coates Carter, added the south porch and vestry. At the same time, the tall and narrow chancel was painted with angels and lilies and an alabaster reredos was installed, carved by William Clarke of Llandaff, with mosaics above by Powell's. The superb tiles are characteristic of Seddon, showing 'Presbyters' offering their crowns. The glass in the east window is by Hardman, c.1879. The stalls, pulpit, lectern and pews are of the date of the building. The hammerbeam roof has carved angels. In the south aisle is a fine portrait medallion of Anna Gallenga (d.1897).

PH

189. LLANFACHES (St Dyfrig), Church in Wales   *Newpt*

Location: in the village off the A48, midway between Chepstow and Newport.
Access: details of key holders advertised in church porch.

A largely fourteenth-century church with a low saddleback west tower, nave, chancel and south porch. The door from the porch into the nave dates from the early seventeenth century. The church was attractively restored in a restrained Arts and Crafts style by Arthur Grove in 1907–8; his are the nave roof, chancel screen and abstract window glazing. The late seventeenth-century stone charity board is extremely unusual.

NY

190. LLANFACHES (Tabernacle), United Reformed Church   *Newpt*

Location: directly on the main A48 road, between Newport and Chepstow south of the village.
Access: service on the second and fourth Sundays of the month at 9.15 a.m. and on the first, third and fifth Sundays at 3 p.m.

Included chiefly for its historical importance as the earliest known Dissenting chapel in Wales, founded in 1639. One expects such an early cause, persecuted for many decades before it could open its doors freely, to be hidden away in a remote mountain valley, but here it is, almost defiantly sitting at the side of the main road into Wales. Founded by William Wroth (1576–1641), the vicar of Llanfaches, who was converted to Puritanism and resigned his living in 1638. Wroth was succeeded by Walter Cradock and, even in the eighteenth century, Dissenters were nicknamed 'Cradociaid'.

The chapel is a small three-bay one-storey block, almost entirely remodelled in the early twentieth century, in a more or less modern Georgian style, lying parallel to the main road behind a neat burial ground, the entrance door being at the east (gable) end beneath a circular window and a tablet stating 'Llanvaches Congregational Chapel 1639'. At an angle to the chapel, at the west end, is the William Wroth Memorial Hall built in 1924.

PM

191. LLANFAIR CILGEDDIN (St Mary the Virgin), formerly Church in Wales, now in the care of the Friends of Friendless Churches

Mons

Location: by itself, some distance from the village, on the B4598, 6 miles south-east of Abergavenny.
Access: kept locked; for details of keyholders ring the Friends Office, telephone: 020 7236 3934.

This small church, reached down winding lanes in the Usk watermeadows, had the good fortune to have as rector from 1872 the Revd W. J. Coussmaker Lindsay. He commissioned John Dando Sedding to restore the church, which he did with great sympathy and sensitivity in 1873–6. The nave, chancel and south porch are basically medieval, but repaired and, where necessary (especially the south wall), reconstructed. The charming bellcote is new. Inside, the font and its cover are late medieval. The medieval screen came from elsewhere. Sedding's furnishings include the simple alabaster and marble reredos, the tiles, the altar rails and the carved timber pulpit. The most memorable feature of the church is the comprehensive scheme of decoration in sgraffito – a technique that involves several layers of plaster of different colours, cut away to make clear and simple pictures. The work was carried out in 1888 in memory of Lindsay's wife. The artist, recommended by Sedding, was Heywood Sumner. The nave panels illustrate the Benedicite, and include sea lions, ploughed fields (with local hills), children with hoops, winged winds and so on. Existing wall tablets are left *in situ*. Over the chancel arch is Christ in majesty. Sedding provided a new shaft and head for the churchyard cross, and the Lindsays have delightful tombstones.

PH

192. LLANGWM UCHAF (St Jerome), Church in Wales

Mons

Location: by itself off the B4235, 3 miles east of Usk.
Access: generally open.

An unusual church, comprising a long nave with a south porch and a short chancel with a tower on the north side, dating from the thirteenth to fifteenth centuries. It was restored between 1863 and 1878 by J. P. Seddon and Ewan Christian. They preserved the magnificent early sixteenth-century rood screen and loft, but otherwise provided an excellent ensemble of contemporary furnishings which have survived intact: octagonal stone font, stone pulpit, wooden lectern, choir stalls and pews, elaborate tiling and stained glass illustrating the Annunciation in the east window.

NY

193. LLANGYFIW (St David), formerly Church in Wales, now in the care of the Friends of Friendless Churches *Mons*

Location: by itself off the A449, 2 miles south-east of Usk.
Access: generally open.

The only Anglican church in the diocese of Monmouth to preserve a complete early nineteenth-century interior: box pews, pulpit, reading desk, altar rails, stone seat against the east wall of the chancel, plastered and boarded roofs and a crude medieval font with wooden cover. The church also preserves substantial fragments of the former medieval rood screen and loft.

NY

194. LLANOVER/LLANOFOR (St Bartholomew), Church in Wales
Mons

Location: between the village and the River Usk on a side road off the A4042, 3 miles south-east of Abergavenny.
Access: Sunday service at 9 a.m.

A fifteenth-century church, preserving its original wagon roof, with a south porch dated 1750. The attractive interior has a number of interesting features and furnishings: a twelfth-century font; eighteenth-century altar rails; an early nineteenth-century Royal Arms over the chancel arch; mid-nineteenth-century pews inscribed with the names of the properties to which they were originally assigned; the Hall family pew made up from the remains of eighteenth-century box pews; hatchments on the north wall of the nave; and the pulpit entered through the wall from the former rood staircase.

NY

195. LLANTHONY/LLANHONDDU (St David), Church in Wales
Mons

Location: next to the priory ruins on a side road off the A465, 10 miles north-west of Abergavenny.
Access: generally open.

The church, next to the extensive ruins of the former priory church, was formed after the priory's dissolution in 1538 by a conversion of the former infirmary and its chapel which dated from the twelfth century. The church was pleasantly restored by J. J. Spencer of Bath in 1886–7 and preserves a simple medieval font and eighteenth-century altar rails. It is also a place of pilgrimage for those visiting the priory ruins and those of Father Ignatius' late Victorian monastery at Capel-y-Ffin (see above) further up the valley.

NY

196. LLANTILIO CROSSENNY/LLANDEILO GRESYNNI

(St Teilo), Church in Wales   *Mons*

Location: by itself near the B4223, 6 miles east of Abergavenny.
Access: generally open.

This large cruciform church with its central tower and broach spire and its aisled nave dates from the thirteenth and fourteenth centuries and was well restored by Prichard and Seddon in 1856–7, although they ignored many of the accepted principles of ecclesiology, for instance by placing the benches across the full width of the nave with no central passageway. The large north chapel, which extends the full length of both the crossing and the chancel, houses an exceptionally fine collection of seventeenth-century carved ledger stones. There is good stained glass by C. E. Kempe, dated between 1887 and 1909, and of 1958–60 by Celtic Studios, in several windows.

NY

197. LLANTILIO PERTHOLEY/LLANDEILO BERTHOLAU

(St Teilo), Church in Wales   *Mons*

Location: by itself off the A465, 2 miles north of Abergavenny.
Access: services on Sundays at 8 a.m., 10.30 a.m. and 6 p.m.

A large and very attractive thirteenth- to sixteenth-century church comprising a nave, chancel, north-west tower, south porch, north and south aisles to the eastern part of the nave and an outer south aisle; this and part of the south aisle have carved wooden arcades. There are excellent ceiled wagon roofs throughout. Two late medieval pews with poppy-heads were bought in as part of a sensitive restoration by Kempson and Fowler in 1890–3. The simple chancel screen and pulpit, incorporating panels of seventeenth-century carved woodwork, also date from this restoration. There is a fifteenth-century font, a poor box date 1704, several eighteenth- and nineteenth-century wall tablets, a benefaction board and painted texts either side of the west window. The excellent modern light fittings of 1974 were designed by George Pace.

NY

198. MAGOR/MAGWYR (St Mary), Church in Wales   *Mons*

Location: in centre of village, 1 mile south of the M4 (junction 23A).
Access: key held at the Christian bookshop in the village.

A large thirteenth- to fifteenth-century church comprising a long chancel, central tower and an aisled nave, the aisles being extended eastwards to flank the tower. The two-storey north porch is particularly handsome. The church was over-restored by John Norton in 1861–8, but the chancel, which is empty apart from the altar raised on a series of steps, has a good medieval roof. The choir stalls are placed under the crossing. The elaborate arcades between the nave and aisles have richly carved capitals and the south-east pillar incorporates a vaulted niche for a statue. The octagonal font dates from the fifteenth century.

NY

199. MALPAS (St Mary), Church in Wales   *Newpt*

Location: on the A4051, 2 miles north of Newport.
Access: services on Sundays at 8 a.m., 9.45 a.m., 11.30 a.m. and 6.30 p.m. and on Wednesdays at 10 a.m.

The architect of the church built in 1849–50 was John Prichard, who – exceptionally for him – used the Norman style. The reason was that it was on the site of the twelfth-century chapel of a Cluniac cell, of which only one corbel could be reused. The square bell turret over the west end echoes the medieval one. Although small, the church is very elaborate. Built of mauve and grey stone, it has a chancel arch ornamented with big dogtooth, based on the original one. The Caen stone font, pulpit and the lectern covered in Romanesque carving are remarkable. Much of the stained glass is by George Rogers of Worcester and is vigorous and colourful. His work includes the triple east window (1850). The west and north-east windows are by Hardman (1860s). The lychgate is also Norman.

PH

200. MATHERN/MERTHYR TEWDRIG (St Tewdrig), Church in Wales *Mons*

Location: beyond the main part of the village, off the A48, 2 miles south-west of Chepstow.
Access: generally open between April and October.

The church forms part of a major architectural group, including the former palace of the bishop of Llandaff, and was largely rebuilt by Bishop John Marshall (1478–96). Apart from the fifteenth-century roofs and fragments of contemporary stained glass in the west window of the south aisle, the interior dates largely from the vigorous restoration by John Pritchard and Ewan Christian between 1880 and 1889. The pulpit, pews and elaborate stone font are by Pritchard and are good examples of the period. In the north and south windows of the chancel is some early Victorian stained glass by Joseph Bell of Bristol, installed between 1848 and 1854, which is among the earliest neo-medievalist stained glass in Wales.

NY

201. MONMOUTH/TREFYNWY (St James), Methodist *Mons*

Location: in town centre.
Access: Sunday service at 10.30 a.m.

Monmouth is a town of good chapels, and this one, formerly the Wesleyan chapel, is discreetly tucked away, almost hidden from St James Street by other buildings. Yet no building deserves to be more prominently displayed since, both inside and out, it is one of the handsomest chapels in Wales. It was designed by the Monmouth architect George Maddox in 1837, and has a fine three-bay pedimented façade, stuccoed and painted in contrasting colours to emphasise its precise classical features. Below the pediment are three round-headed Georgian windows with shell arcading between Ionic pilasters, while the ground floor has two pedimented square windows both sides of an elegant projecting porch standing on four fluted Ionic pillars.

The interior continues in the same style, with fine Georgian windows throughout and galleries around three sides of the church carried on Ionic columns. There is a bow-fronted pulpit with elegant stairs. The floor level of the chapel was raised by 2 feet in 1885, which unfortunately had the effect of burying the bases of the columns, but otherwise this is a most satisfying building, clearly showing the wealth of the congregation and their good taste and sense in putting the whole project into the hands of a professional architect.

PM

202. MONMOUTH/TREFYNWY (St Mary), Church in Wales *Mons*

Location: in town centre.
Access: generally open during the summer.

The former priory church was consecrated in 1101. After the dissolution of the monastery in 1536 the nave was restored for use as a parish church but was, apart from the fourteenth-century west tower and spire, rebuilt by Francis Smith of Warwick in 1736–7. This church was, in turn, completely remodelled by G. E. Street, with a new chancel, in 1881–3. The spacious interior has stained glass by C. E. Kempe, installed in 1882–8, a reredos painting of the Adoration of the Kings by Watney Wilson (1888), screens by W. D. Caröe, and good Anglo-Catholic furnishings including Stations of the Cross on slate panels and a modern statue of Our Lady. A rare, but exceptionally important, survival is the fine set of fifteenth-century floor tiles in the baptistery. As befits the parish church of a historic county town, there is a good collection of eighteenth- and nineteenth-century memorial tablets on the walls.

NY

203. MONMOUTH/TREFYNWY (St Thomas), Church in Wales

Mons

Location: in a western suburb of Monmouth close to the bridge over the Monnow.
Access: generally open.

The parish church of Overmonnow was built as a chapel of ease in the twelfth century and given its present status when the nave was largely rebuilt by Arthur Wyatt and Matthew Beasen in 1830–1. The nave retains furnishings of this date. In the western part of the nave the seating is in two blocks with a central passageway; in the eastern part there is a central block of seating with side passageways and stalls along the side walls. At the western end of the south stall block is a neo-Norman font with a tall wooden cover. The gallery across the west end of the nave has been extended across the north and south walls to form canopies over the stalls underneath. In 1874–5 the central pulpit and reading desk were removed when the twelfth-century chancel was restored and refurnished under the direction of John Prichard.

NY

204. NASH (St Mary), Church in Wales

Newpt

Location: in village on a side road off the A48, 3 miles south-east of Newport.
Access: generally open but key kept at neighbouring house.

The church comprises a fifteenth-century north-east tower and spire, a barn-like nave of c.1800 and a chancel of 1861 by J. P. Seddon. The contrast between the nave and chancel is extraordinary. The former retains its complete furnishings of c.1800 with high, square box pews, three-decker pulpit and a west gallery for singers and musicians. The chancel is stalled for a surpliced choir and has the customary Tractarian accoutrements.

NY

205. NEWBRIDGE/CEFNBYCHAN (Our Lady of Peace), Roman Catholic *Torfaen*

Location: on the A467, 8 miles north-west of Newport.
Access: The church is currently under repair and is not generally open at the present time, though there is Mass on Sundays at 6 p.m. After the completion of the repairs the church will be accessible through a new visitor centre.

The white-painted campanile up on the hillside above the Ebbw Valley strikes an exotic note. The church was built in 1939–40, hence the dedication. It was paid for by the Hon. Mrs Fflorens Roch, daughter of Lord Treowen of Llanarth Court. Her architect was Philip Dalton Hepworth, educated at the École des Beaux Arts, Paris, and at the British School at Rome, and best known as a domestic architect. The church has a strongly Italian flavour: the walls are rendered and painted white, the roofs are pantiled and the campanile has round-arched openings at the top with balconies. The matching presbytery is east of the church. The interior is impressively tall and light. The roof has charming painted decoration. The fittings are influenced by Art Deco: they include the iron screen at the west end, the travertine font in its polygonal baptistery and – most memorable of all – the amazing electoliers.

PH

206. NEWPORT/CASNEWYDD (Cathedral of St Gwynllyw *alias* Woolos), Church in Wales *Newpt*

Location: in city centre.
Access: open daily, 9 a.m.–5 p.m.

When the new diocese of Monmouth was formed in 1921 consideration was given to raising either this building, the former monastic churches at Abergavenny, Chepstow or Monmouth (see above), or even a re-roofed Tintern Abbey, to cathedral status; a decision in favour of Newport was not made until 1949. It is an unusual building. A long thirteenth-century narthex links the fifteenth-century west tower to the remarkable twelfth-century nave, with its handsome arcades and west doorway, and its aisles rebuilt in the fifteenth century. In 1960–4 the short chancel was quadrupled in length by an extension designed by A. D. R. Caröe. Although the view of the east end through the narthex is impressive the detail of both the nineteenth- and twentieth-century furnishings disappoints. Even the reredos and rose window above it, by John Piper and Patrick Reyntiens, lack either colour or power. As part of the work on the cathedral in the 1960s much of the Victorian stained glass was removed, including work by Hardman, with only the central figures being retained against a background of clear glass. The few surviving medieval monuments in St Mary's Chapel have all been severely mutilated.

NY

207. PONTYPOOL (Crane Street Church), Baptist   *Torfaen*

Location: in town centre.

Access: open on Mondays, Wednesdays and Fridays, 10 a.m.–2 p.m. during the summer.

Crane Street Baptist church is only three bays wide, and directly on a street in the centre of Pontypool, but it has the monumentality of a Greek temple, an excellent example of neo-classical revival architecture, designed by Aaron Crossfield in 1847, with improvements by J. H. Langdon. The front is of Bath stone ashlar, dominated by a Greek Doric temple portico, with two pillars and two square antae supporting the central pediment. Neo-Greek architects imagined that Greek temples were solely lit from the sky, and the original design must have been quite extraordinary, and it is still dominated by light pouring down from its glass roof. The pulpit seems to be of 1847, and the slender square piers holding up the wallplate seem to be neo-classical, but most of the furnishings come from enlargements of 1868 by A. O. Watkins (of Newport), and the fine galleries on all four sides were inserted in 1881. New windows were installed in 1908, and these are in a Perpendicular style decorated with Art Nouveau glass, and there are two of them most disconcertingly to be seen both sides of the Greek Doric entrance. Inside, there is a fine sculpted monument with profile busts to Thomas Thomas (d.1881) and his wife by the Welsh sculptor J. Milo Griffith. Thomas was principal of the Baptist College at Pontypool, and father of the artist T. H. Thomas, 'Arlunydd Penygarn'.

PM

208. PONTYPOOL (Tabernacle), Baptist   *Torfaen*

Location: in the centre of the town of Pontypool take direction (north) marked Trevethin and Penygarn, and halfway up the hill turn sharp left up a one-way street off Penygarn Road, follow the road uphill again for almost a quarter of a mile and the chapel is on the left, set back a few yards from the road.
Access: Sunday service at 11 a.m.

This is one of the earliest Baptist chapels in Wales, built in 1727, and still retains the feel and look of a vernacular farmhouse, still rural although the suburbs of Pontypool have crept up and around it. It is a good place to visit in order to understand the utterly un-churchlike 'meeting-house' quality of so much early Dissenting architecture. A little stone-walled drive leads in from the road towards the (modern) vestry behind the church. A square lime-washed two-storey stone building, it has four twelve-pane sash windows (unfortunately, they are modern replacements protected by grilles), with a small porch (dated 1925) in the centre. There is a splendid roof of stone tiles. There are similar twelve-pane windows at the rear elevation with an immense buttress sustaining the wall. Towards the north and west there is a very large burial ground, with many early gravestones. Some of the earliest are just in front of the chapel porch, the most prominent being a Victorian red granite column of 1863 to the wife of John Probyn, a maltster of Pontypool, which suggests that teetotalism had not reached this area at that date. The interior is greatly altered since 1727 but there is an early nineteenth-century pulpit and box pews, and a good deal of modern stained glass (possibly from the 1930s) in the windows.

PM

209. SKENFRITH/YNYSGYNWRAIDD (St Brigid), Church in Wales

Mons

Location: in village on the B4521, 12 miles north-east of Abergavenny and 8 miles north-west of Monmouth.
Access: generally open.

A large thirteenth-century church with a sixteenth-century south chapel lightly restored by E. G. Davies in 1896. The squat west tower has a wooden belfry. Among the church's treasures are two sixteenth-century carved family pews, an altar tomb of 1557 and a remarkable velvet cope of c.1500 displayed in a special frame. The high altar comprises a medieval mensa on new stone supports, with the seventeenth-century altar table now placed in the south aisle. The Ten Commandments formerly painted on the east wall of the chancel were replaced by exact copies, in frames on the north wall, in 1910.

NY

210. USK/BRYNBUGA (St Mary), Church in Wales

Mons

Location: in town centre.
Access: open daily, 8.30 a.m.–5.30 p.m.

What remains is the central tower, nave and north aisle of the former priory church. The tower is twelfth century, the nave and aisle fifteenth century, with two elaborate porches. The chief feature of the interior is the magnificent fifteenth-century rood screen and loft. There is also a fine brass of c.1400 with an inscription in Welsh, a handsome organ case of 1862 formerly in Llandaff Cathedral and an eighteenth-century pulpit, the canopy of which is now being used as a font cover. In the south porch is a large painted board of 1726 showing the seating plan of the church, and the names of the pew holders, at that date.

NY

6. Medieval stained glass window (Anna and Joachim), Gresford, All Saints. *Martin Crampin*

7. West window by Burne-Jones, Hawarden, St Deiniol. *Martin Crampin*

9. Llanbedr Dyffryn Clwyd, St Peter. *Martin Crampin*

10. Pentrobin, St John the Baptist. *Martin Crampin*

11. Amlwch, Our Lady Star of the Sea and St Winefride. *Martin Crampin*

15. Ceiling fresco of Christ Pantokrator, Cardiff, St Nicholas. Martin Crampin

18. Restored medieval church at St Fagan's from Llandeilo Talybont, St Teilo. *St Fagans: National History Museum*

21. St Davids Cathedral. *Martin Crampin*

6

Churches and Chapels in South-West Wales

211. ALLTYFERIN/PONTARGOTHI (Holy Trinity), Church in Wales

Carms

Location: off the A40, 7 miles north-west of Carmarthen.

Access: open on Thursdays, May–September, 2 p.m.–4 p.m.

Henry James Bath, of Alltyferin, was wealthy from shipping and copper in the Swansea Valley, and he paid for this delightful little church, begun in 1865. It was not completed until 1878, three years after his death. It was intended to provide English services, as the parish church at Llanegwad had only Welsh ones. The architect was Benjamin Bucknall, best known for Woodchester Park in Gloucestershire. It was his last building before he retired to Algiers. Externally, the church is quite simple, of sandstone with Bath dressings. The windows are round headed except for the plate-traceried east one. The wood and slate *flèche* is charming. The rich interior comes as a surprise. The fine wall paintings were executed by A. Stansell of Taunton. There are twenty-five biblical stories, and the chancel dado represents green fabric hangings – a subject about which Bucknall published a book. The wooden barrel vault is also prettily decorated. The reredos is of alabaster and Bath stone. The brass lectern is supported by an angel. The stained glass is by Clayton and Bell: the west windows show the founder holding the church, and his widow and nephew who completed it.

PH

212. BAYVIL/BEIFIL (St Andrew), formerly Church in Wales, now in the care of the Friends of Friendless Churches *Pembs*

Location: by itself off the B4582, 7 miles south-west of Cardigan.
Access: key at neighbouring farmhouse.

A delightful early nineteenth-century chapel of ease, retaining its original fittings, carefully restored in *c.*1980 by Roger Clive-Powell. The furnishings comprise a canopied three-decker pulpit, the clerk's desk being placed to the east of the pulpit and the reading desk to the west, box pews, clear glass and a raised sanctuary with the original rails but a later altar table. The original altar table now stands at the west end of the nave.

NY

213. CAERFARCHELL (Chapel), Calvinistic Methodist *Pembs*

Location: in village, off the A487, 2 miles north-east of St Davids.
Access: service every Sunday at 2 p.m.

A very attractive, almost square, chapel of 1827 with a hipped roof. Inside, the five-sided panelled gallery, supported on wooden pillars, and its simple benches are original. The rest of the chapel was expensively refurnished in the late nineteenth century with a large pulpit and *sêt-fawr* on the entrance wall, and pews with doors angled to face them. The communion table is placed beneath the pulpit within the *sêt-fawr*.

NY

214. CALDEY (Abbey Church of St Mary and St Samson), Roman Catholic *Pembs*

Location: on island, accessible by boat from Tenby.
Access: visitors may attend the daily offices in the church and also Mass on Sundays at 10.45 a.m. The monastery is closed to visitors.

A masterpiece by an unsung architect, the Abbey of St Mary and St Samson is one of the outstanding church buildings of Wales. Originally built for the Anglican Benedictine community who came to

19. Caldey Island, Abbey of St Mary and St Samson. *Martin Crampin*

Caldey in 1906, the monastic range includes the church and chapter house (1910), the abbot's house (1912; now guesthouse) and the cloister (1910–15). The layout of the abbey was conceived by Abbot Aelred Carlyle with the assistance of Br Jerome Hawes, a member of the 1906 community, and executed by the architect John Coates Carter. Continental inspiration is often inferred from the series of towers and turrets, as well as the terracotta roof tiles, which give the building an Italianate air. In fact, the design appears chiefly a mixture of Welsh and English vernacular features with some structures directly copied from medieval British models – for example, the kitchen, which is modelled on the abbot's kitchen at Glastonbury. The Benedictine community became Roman Catholic in 1913 and sold the island in 1928 to the Cistercian order, which owns the abbey today.

The abbey church (1910) is Romanesque in form with a square tower to the south side, timber roof, round arches and wheel window at the east end. The chancel is at the western end, an arrangement necessitated by the orientation of the monastic range. The exterior is white rough cast with limestone feature blocks and terracotta tiled roof. The interior of the church as originally built was panelled and decorated in ornate style – the abbot's chapel in the guesthouse (not accessible to the general public) retains some original interior decoration. The interior was rebuilt in 1950, after the church had been gutted by fire in 1940, in austere style consistent with the Cistercian ideal. The hammerbeam roof and choir stalls are in dark wood, while the bare walls are of plain cream with small clerestory windows – round in the chancel and arched in nave and narthex. A wrought-iron crucifix is framed by the plain round arch of the apse. The closeness of the nave and gallery to the choir allows full enjoyment of the monastic office.

JW

215. CALDEY (St David), Roman Catholic   *Pembs*

Location: a short distance from the Abbey Church.
Access: generally open.

The parish church of Caldey Island, St David's is a two-cell structure of early second-millennium date, standing in a probably more ancient burial ground. Less heavily used than the Abbey Church, it is a quiet haven for contemplation and private prayer. The church was probably the *Sancta Maria super maris litus* referred to by William Worcestre (the current dedication dates from the early 1900s); it originally stood on the shore of an inlet, now silted up. The graves visible today are all from the early twentieth century onwards, but medieval cist burials run south of the church and extend beyond the current churchyard wall, suggesting that it is an earlier church site.

The church was restored to ecclesiastical use in 1838 by Cabot Kynaston, after a period of domestic use. The west door of two plain orders is around thirteenth century in date, giving access to a sparsely decorated interior with stripped walls. The imposts of the chancel arch suggest a twelfth-century date. In 1923–5, John Coates Carter replaced the pointed Neo-Gothic nave windows of 1838 with the paired lancets seen today. Stained glass windows (1922–4) by Dom Theodore Bailey, a member of the Benedictine community in the 1920s, which include the famous Fish (east wall of chancel) and Tree of Life (west gable) windows, give a powerful sense of colour to the plain interior. The font in Portland stone is by Eric Gill. The church was Anglican from 1838 but became Roman Catholic in 1913.

JW

216. CALDEY (St Illtyd's Priory), Roman Catholic   *Pembs*

Location: a short walk from the Abbey Church.
Access: generally open.

An atmospheric combination of medieval and modern, St Illtyd's is the chapel of the medieval Tironian priory of Caldey, founded around 1120–30. Substantial elements of the east and west ranges of the cloister garth survive, the whole until recently incorporated into a Georgian mansion (now demolished) which lay to the north. The dedication to St Illtyd is modern, the medieval dedication being to St Mary.

St Illtyd's is a two-cell structure located, unusually for a Benedictine house, on the south side of the cloister – the mother house of Tiron has the same arrangement. Entrance is through a tower of probably fourteenth-century date with leaning spire, giving access to a rectangular narthex, timber-roofed nave and sanctuary with pointed stone vault. The sanctuary still has the monks' doorway into the dormitory. The fine trefoil piscina and roll-moulded east window of the chancel are of around thirteenth-century date, though the low ceiling appears of later date.

As seen today, with its dark interior and brightly coloured windows, St Illtyd's is a uniquely preserved example both of a small medieval priory church and of Victorian/Edwardian Anglo-Catholic restoration. The interior was restored (1897–9) by William Done Bushell (owner of the island from 1894 to 1906). The dado with ornate decoration (c.1897–8) is by William Egerton Hine, then art master at Harrow. The stalls were a gift of the Anglican Cowley Fathers in 1906. The window in the south wall of the nave, depicting St Illtyd, is by Dom Theodore Bailey (1922), a member of the Benedictine community in the 1920s. An ECM with incised cross, fifth-/sixth-century Irish Ogham inscription and later Latin text stands on the south side of the nave. The chapel has been Roman Catholic since 1913.

JW

217. CAREW CHERITON (St Mary), Church in Wales   *Pembs*

Location: by itself off the A477, 3 miles north-east of Pembroke.
Access: generally open.

An impressive late medieval church with a handsome west tower. Inside, there is an important group of thirteenth- to eighteenth-century monuments and a fine collection of medieval floor tiles. Shields and Tudor roses are carved on the arcades and capitals. The nave and aisles were restored by David Brandon in 1856 and retain a complete set of contemporary pews with doors. The chancel was restored by W. D. Caröe in 1908–10, but the excellent high altar and reredos were designed by John Coates Carter in 1923. There is also good stained glass of 1879 by Alexander Gibbs in the east window of the chancel. In the churchyard is a seventeenth-century schoolroom with a cellar, used as a charnel house, underneath.

NY

218. CARMARTHEN/CAERFYRDDIN (St Peter), Church in Wales
Carms

Location: in town centre at the east end of King Street.
Access: services on Sundays at 8 a.m., 11 a.m. and 4.30 p.m. and on Wednesdays at 10.30 a.m.

A large town church dating largely from the fourteenth century with a sixteenth-century west tower, attractively lime rendered in 2002. Internally, the church was much altered by its heavy restoration under the direction of R. K. Penson in 1856–8. This was, however, in some respects, remarkably conservative. He retained the seating arrangements, pews with doors and poppy-heads, and the separate mayoral and vicarage pews, of 1851–5, and the west gallery of 1789 with its organ of 1793. Other important surviving furnishings include a canopied pew of 1709 at the west end of the nave and two former altar tables, a wooden one of 1716 and a black marble one of 1829. The consistory court with its episcopal chair, table and pews, dates from Penson's restoration. The chancel and east end of the nave was refurnished in 1882–92 with a new pulpit, eagle lectern, reredos and choir stalls. Among the large collection of monuments is the tomb of Sir Rhys ap Thomas (d.1525) and the wall tablet to Lady Anne Vaughan (d.1672).

NY

219. CARMARTHEN/CAERFYRDDIN (Capel Heol Awst), Independent *Carms*

Location: in town centre at the west end of Lammas Street.
Access: services on Sundays at 10 a.m and 3.30 p.m.

The congregation was established in the late seventeenth century and for many years the minister acted as the principal of Carmarthen's important Dissenting academy. The present chapel dates from 1826–7 and the attached Sunday school from 1888–9. Both have preserved their original furnishings virtually intact. The chapel has a handsome plaster ceiling and galleries, supported on iron columns painted to look like marble, with tiered seating. The tall wine-glass pulpit is supported on a wooden pedestal. The ground-floor seating is provided by box pews and there are two small Gothick windows containing eighteenth-century painted glass in the vestibule screen. The Sunday school also has a handsome galleried interior.

NY

220. CARMARTHEN/CAERFYRDDIN (English Baptist Chapel), Baptist *Carms*

Location: in town centre at the east end of Lammas Street.
Access: open on Wednesdays, 10 a.m.–2.30 p.m.

Externally, one of the most impressive of the many late nineteenth-century chapels in the region, its elaborate classical portico is set well back from the street. It was designed by one of its deacons, George Morgan, in 1869–70 and has a largely unaltered interior. There is a gallery, with tiered seating, across the entrance wall. On the ground floor are three blocks of pews with doors. The low pulpit is railed on a platform over the baptistery with the organ placed behind the pulpit. The windows are filled with coloured glass.

NY

221. CHERITON (St Catwg), Church in Wales — *Swan.*

Location: on a minor road at the north-east end of Cheriton village at the west end of the Gower peninsula.
Access: key available at the cottage (pottery) across the road to the east of the churchyard.

The church stands in a shallow combe hidden from the village and from Landimore marshes half a mile to the north. It is said to have been built here when the sea threatened the previous church at Landimore. The little building, dumpy but robust, has a crossing tower as wide as the chancel and a slightly wider nave with a south porch. The transeptal north vestry was added in 1874–5.

The tower has a defensive air, with slit windows and the typical Glamorgan crown of a gabled roof rising behind corbelled battlements. What make the church special are the Early English style details, simplified versions of those found in the early thirteenth-century parts of Llandaff Cathedral. Most impressive is the south doorway with its shaft rings and stiff-leaf foliage capitals. Most unusual are the two double-chamfered arches which support the tower and rest on corbels, one carved with a stiff-leaf sprig, another with a grotesque head. The lancets in the chancel with cusped-ogee heads are early fourteenth century in form, but may be part of the works carried out in 1874–5 for the Revd J. D. Davies, to his own design. The nave roof bosses, the altar rail and choir stalls are said to have been carved by him.

JN

222. CILYCWM (St Michael), Church in Wales   *Carms*

Location: in the village approached by side roads off either the A483 or
A482, 4 miles north-west of Llandovery.
Access: generally open.

A handsome fifteenth-century double-naved church with a north-west
tower; this has an unusual staircase with an external entrance and a
window into the nave. The interior was lightly restored by W. D. Caröe in
1904–6. He preserved the plaster-vaulted porch under the tower and the
original barrel roof to the south nave. The important wall paintings, dated
1724 and 1795, include the Royal Arms, Ten Commandments, Creed,
Moses and a skeleton figure of death. The other furnishings are by Caröe
and are extremely attractive.

NY

223. EGLWYS GYMYN (St Margaret Marloes), Church in Wales

Carms

Location: by itself on the B4314 between Pendine and Red Roses,
5 miles south-west of St Clears.
Access: Sunday service at 10 a.m.

This simple little church is remarkable for its rough-stone vaulted nave
roof, and the simple round arch cut in the massive wall between nave
and chancel. The east and west windows date from 1848, and the other
windows and bellcote are of 1856 by Thomas David. The chancel was
largely rebuilt in 1877–8 by Clapton Crabb Rolfe of Oxford. The church is,
however, chiefly memorable for the restoration carried out in 1899–1902
for the Society for the Protection of Ancient Buildings, under the auspices
of George Gilbert Treherne, steward of the Lordship of Laugharne. The
architect was William Weir, but he worked under the direction of Philip
Webb. The new timber fittings are simple and solid. The lectern, with a
figure of St Margaret, was designed in 1903 by George Jack, and carved
by Laurence Turner. There are several beautiful windows by F. C. Eden,
with delicate detail (1906–17), and note also the painted wooden board

of patrons (1911). On the north wall of the nave are wall paintings, dating from the thirteenth to the seventeenth centuries, of patterns and texts. A fifth- or sixth-century ECM (found by Treherne) is inscribed in both Latin (*Avitoria filia Cunigni*) and Ogham and is enclosed at the west end in some deliberately primitive woodwork designed by Philip Webb. The churchyard cross, in memory of Treherne, dates from 1926 (by T. G. Clarke of Llandaff) and the lychgate from 1930.

PH

224. FISHGUARD/ABERGWAUN (Hermon Chapel), Baptist

Pembs

Location: in town centre.
Access: services on Sundays at 10 a.m. and 6 p.m. and on Thursdays at 2.30 p.m.

A very handsome classical chapel of 1832, set back from the street, with an elaborate portico incorporating the staircases to the galleries at each side of the entrance. The original box pews, tiered against the entrance and side walls and in the galleries, have been preserved. The pulpit is also original but the communion enclosure over the baptistery has been enlarged. The chapel was extended in 1906 to provide space for an organ and choir in a new railed gallery behind the pulpit, and beyond that a new large vestry and Sunday schoolroom.

NY

225. GARNANT (Old Bethel Chapel), Independent   *Carms*

Location: by itself off the A474, 3 miles north-east of Ammanford.
Access: available by contacting Mr J. G. Thomas (telephone: 01269 822160).

A delightful and completely unaltered chapel of 1825 in a rural setting in the Amman Valley. The wine-glass pulpit, family pew and communion enclosure are placed against the entrance wall and there is a fireplace on the opposite wall. Between them are box pews. There are galleries on three sides of the interior with tiered benches. The walls are lined with hat pegs and lighting is provided by candles only. The chapel is used only once a year, for an early morning service of *Plygain* on Christmas Day.

NY

226. HAVERFORDWEST/HWLFFORDD (St Mary), Church in Wales *Pembs*

Location: in town centre.
Access: generally open.

The largest of the three medieval churches in the town, although built on a very confined site. Dating from the thirteenth to the fifteenth centuries, the church comprises a nave with north aisle, chancel with north chapel, north and south porches and a north-west tower. The arcade between the nave and north aisle has very elaborately carved capitals. The church retains its fifteenth-century roofs and two carved bench ends, one illustrating the triumph of St Michael over Satan. There have been several restorations, by Thomas Rowlands in 1844, W. H. Lindsey and C. E. Giles in the 1860s, Ewan Christian in the 1880s and, finally, W. D. Caröe in 1903–5. The choir stalls are by Christian, the pulpit and pews by Caröe. The stained glass in the east window by C. E. Kempe dates from 1893. As befits a major town church, there is a large collection of monuments, many dating from the seventeenth and eighteenth centuries, including ones signed by the fashionable London sculptors, Thomas Burnell and Christopher Horsnaile.

NY

227. HAVERFORDWEST/HWLFFORDD (Tabernacle Chapel), Independent *Pembs*

Location: in town centre.
Access: on Fridays, 10.30 a.m.–12.30 p.m. when a drop-in club is held in the schoolroom.

An attractive chapel of 1774 with a bow-fronted entrance portico painted blue and white. The chapel was enlarged and the interior

20. Pew-end carving (late fifteenth century), Haverfordwest, St Michael.
Martin Crampin

refurnished in 1874. It comprises a five-bay aisled nave with an apse behind the pulpit platform. The ceiling over the nave is coved and those over the aisles are flat. The roof and wrought-iron galleries are supported by iron columns with elaborate capitals. There is similar wrought-iron work in the pulpit and communion enclosure. The seating comprises three blocks of pews with doors in the body of the chapel and tiered seating in the galleries. There is an organ in the gallery across the entrance wall. The apse has several small windows filled with stained glass, either texts or lilies and vines. The adjacent schoolroom dates from 1864 and the wrought-iron entrance gate from 1835.

NY

228. KIDWELLY/CYDWELI (St Mary), Church in Wales   *Carms*

Location: in town centre.
Access: generally open.

A former priory church, dating largely from the fourteenth and fifteenth centuries. It is a cruciform building with a north-west tower and spire and an exceptionally broad nave and chancel, heavily restored by 1885–9. Earlier furnishings include the 1713 door to the tower with a Latin inscription 'haec est domus Dei porta caeli' and the organ case of 1762, formerly at St Mary's, Swansea. To the right of the east window is a delicate fifteenth-century elaborate carving of the Virgin and Child. There is striking modern stained glass (Celtic Studios, 1960) in the west window.

NY

229. LAUGHARNE/TALACHARN (St Martin), Church in Wales
Carms

Location: set back from the main road on the approach to the town from St Clears.
Access: generally open.

A large cruciform church, with a central tower, dating from the fourteenth and fifteenth centuries. Major restorations were carried out by R. K. Penson in 1853–7 and again in 1872–6. Penson, however, restored the medieval reredos, the only one surviving in south-west Wales, and in 1901 it was filled with new statues by Bridgeman of Lichfield. Another important and successful addition to the interior was the new rood screen and loft, by C. E. Ponting, installed in 1909. There is much stained glass by William Wailes dating from the 1850s and 1860s.

NY

230. LLANDEILO (St Teilo), Church in Wales   *Carms*

Location: in town centre.

Access: open Easter–October, Tuesdays–Saturdays, 11a.m.–4 p.m.

Apart from the sixteenth-century west tower, restored by Ewan Christian in 1883, the church was rebuilt in 1848–50 under the direction of Sir George Gilbert Scott. It comprises a nave, north aisle, south transept, north porch and chancel. In 1979 the aisle was walled off and later subdivided to form a series of rooms for meetings or social events. The pulpit, pews and font are by Scott but the chancel was refurnished with a reredos of 1895 and choir stalls of 1905. In the church are two tenth-century cross-heads and a large number of later monuments. These include a fine Neo-Gothic brass to a former vicar and unsuccessful candidate for a Welsh bishopric, the Revd John Griffiths, who died in 1878.

NY

231. LLANDELOY (St Teilo), formerly Church in Wales, now in the care of the Friends of Friendless churches   *Pembs*

Location: in village on a side road between the A487 and B4330, 6 miles north-west of St Davids.

Access: generally open.

This low and simple church had been in ruins since the 1840s. Rebuilding took place in 1925–6, to the design of John Coates Carter, formerly pupil, assistant and partner of J. P. Seddon. He gave his services freely. The fabric of the church was carefully restored to 'what it most likely was at the beginning of the sixteenth century', the date of its latest feature, the roof stair. The leaning west wall was ingeniously jacked up straight. The chancel is at a marked angle to the nave and there is a transeptal chapel on the south, linked to the chancel by a diagonal passage. The exterior, of dark rubble, is quite plain, with only a simple bellcote for emphasis. The interior is dominated by the scissor-truss roofs and the roof screen, loft and pulpit, of carved oak. The two altars are of stone, as is the medieval font. Floors, stoup and piscinae are slate. The most individualistic of the furnishings is the reredos, a gesso-and-tempera panel in a carved frame, probably painted by Carter himself. It shows St John the Divine, Pembroke Dock, whose vicar, Archdeacon David Prosser, was its donor, and St David's Cathedral, linked by the sun, the moon and a rainbow. The stained glass in the east and transept windows is probably by R. J. Newbery.

PH

232. LLANELLI (Capel Als), Independent *Carms*

Location: prominently sited at junction of Wern Road and Als Street just to the east of the town centre.
Access: Sunday services at 10.30 a.m. and at 3 p.m. (winter) or 6 p.m. (summer).

Llanelli was a town dominated by its chapels, Capel Als being the most famous, because of its long association with the famous Independent preacher, the Revd David Rees (1801–69), founder and editor of *Y Diwygiwr* (The Reformer), the journal symbolising the politicisation of the Nonconformists, and who is commemorated by a Gothic marble wall tablet to the left of the pulpit. The highly unusual chapel name comes from the cottage on the site belonging to one Alice, the location being one of huge potential, since it was at the hub of Llanelli's industrial activity, the meeting place of roads and railways at the east end of the town. A marble tablet in the outer vestibule records the foundation of the chapel in 1780 and its many reconstructions, the present being a remodelling in 1894–5 (the architect was a former ship's carpenter, Owen Morris Roberts of Porthmadog) of a square classical box of 1852 by the Revd Thomas Thomas, 'Tomos Glan-Dwr'. The 1894–5 chapel cost £4,995.

The stuccoed Victorian classical chapel façade is five bays wide, with round-arched windows, classical pilasters and a small pediment inscribed 'Capel Als', with two corner pavilions containing staircases. On the ground floor, both sides of the entrance doors, are two small pentagonal porches and a veranda stretching between them. The interior, with seating for 1,100 persons, is lavishly furnished, with galleries around the four sides of the chapel, the whole dominated by a Bishop organ of 1880, which, apparently, was paid for in 200 gold sovereigns, which the bishop representative carried in a bag to London. The windows at the front of the chapel depict musical instruments, and one of the three windows at the rear of the chapel depicts three musicians of the congregation.

PM

233. LLANGENNYDD (St Cennydd)   *Swan.*

Location: at the western end of the Gower peninsula, 15 miles west of Swansea.
Access: generally open.

This is the largest church in Gower, founded in c.1106–15 by Henry of Warwick, lord of Gower. Llangennydd was an alien priory of the Benedictine community of St Taurin at Evreux. The fabric is largely medieval, with a massive plain saddleback tower (thirteenth century) in transeptual location on the north side of the nave, presumably balancing a range which once stood to the south. The tower is entered from the nave through a pointed arch; a blocked east door may have led to a chapel. The monk's entrance on the south side of the chancel is still visible.

JW

234. LLANGUNNOR/LLANGYNNWR (St Ceinwen), Church in Wales
Carms

Location: on its own off the B4300, just over a mile east of Carmarthen.
Access: services on Sundays at 8 a.m. and 10.45 a.m.

A very attractive double-naved church dating from the fourteenth and fifteenth centuries, interestingly altered during the nineteenth century. In 1815, the arcade between the two naves was replaced by Tuscan columns and, in 1870, the church was, incredibly conservatively, refurnished with box pews now painted dove-grey. Other interesting, and possibly contemporary, survivals are the painted boards inscribed with the Ten Commandments, Creed and Lord's Prayer in Welsh. The chancel was refurnished in limed oak by A. D. R. Caröe in 1960–1. There is a good collection of eighteenth- and nineteenth-century wall tablets, including one in wood and others in slate.

NY

235. MANORBIER (St James), Church in Wales   *Pembs*

Location: slightly away from the village and opposite the castle, off the A4139, 6 miles south-west of Tenby.
Access: generally open between April and September.

A large thirteenth- to fifteenth-century church with an exceptionally thin tower. Nave, aisles, transepts and south porch all have crude stone vaults similar to those of churches in Brittany and the Channel Islands. The fifteenth-century rood loft, a rare survival, was moved to the north aisle during F. Wehnert's restoration of 1865–8. There is also a magnificent Royal Arms of 1702. Most of the furnishings are by Wehnert and include the chancel screen, pulpit (entered through the screen) and choir stalls. Another rare survival is an early nineteenth-century teacher's desk from the former church school.

NY

236. MANORDEIFI (St David), formerly Church in Wales, now in the care of the Friends of Friendless Churches   *Pembs*

Location: on its own near the River Teifi on a side road off the B4332, 5 miles west of Newcastle Emlyn.
Access: generally open.

The simple medieval church, with nave, chancel, west porch and bellcote, was replaced by a new building, nearer the hamlet of Abercych in 1899. The old church preserves its pre-Victorian interior, although the present arrangement of the furnishings dates from a very conservative restoration in 1847. The two-decker pulpit, formerly in the middle of the north wall of the nave, was broken up and moved so that the pulpit and the reading desk now stand one each side of the chancel arch. The seating is provided by a mix of box pews, including two family pews with fireplaces, and open benches. The chancel is empty apart from the altar table, raised on a stone platform and railed on three sides. The font dates from the twelfth century. There are several monuments to the leading families in the parish both inside the church and against its walls in the churchyard.

NY

237. MARTLETWY (Burnett's Hill Chapel), formerly Calvinistic Methodist, now managed by a local trust — *Pembs*

Location: on its own south-west of the village of Martletwy, off the A4075, 10 miles south-west of Narberth.
Access: generally open.

The chapel was built in 1813 and rescued from a state of dereliction by the Pembrokeshire Coast National Park Authority in 2001. Originally, the pulpit was placed on one of the long walls, with the seating arranged to face it, but in *c*.1850 the interior was reorientated, with the pulpit placed on the short wall opposite the entrance, on an unusual raised *sêt-fawr*. Steeply raked benches face the pulpit with hat pegs along the walls. There is no gallery.

NY

238. MORRISTON (Tabernacl), Independent — *Swan.*

Location: on the east side of Woodfield Street, the main shopping street of Morriston, which itself stands west of the main dual carriageway linking the M4 and the centre of Swansea.
Access: entrance through the vestry door on Tuesdays and Wednesdays, 10 a.m.–12 noon, and also Thursdays, 2 p.m.–4 p.m.

Tabernacl is the largest and grandest chapel in Wales, long known as 'The Cathedral of Welsh Nonconformity', designed and built in 1872–3 by the architect John Humphrey of Morriston, at the behest of local tinplate manufacturers, the best known being Daniel Edwards. It dwarfs all the other chapels and churches in the area, and its unusual clock tower and spire can be seen from miles around.

The architect, builders and deacons travelled far and wide to look for inspiration, and its style is an eclectic mixture of classical and Lombardic, the materials used being rock-faced local brown sandstone with a great deal of Bath stone detailing. The three-bay façade is dominated by four pairs of gigantic Corinthian columns, the doors and windows being round headed, the pediment having a round window in the centre, the right flanking bay being the square base of an immense clock tower, with two octagonal storeys rising to a spire, again of an eclectic mixture of classical pilasters and round-headed arches, the clock being between the two octagonal storeys.

The interior is contemporary, and lavishly fitted, with very broad galleries right around the chapel – its seating capacity is about 1,450; its most striking feature is the way the gallery swoops dramatically down towards the pulpit, to accommodate a large choir beneath the organ, which has not only a central pipe case, but also two side cases like huge corner cupboards, all with Gothic timber casing.

PM

239. MYDDFAI (St Michael), Church in Wales   *Carms*

Location: in village approached by side roads off the A40 and A4069, 4 miles south-east of Llandovery.
Access: generally open.

A large double-naved fifteenth-century church with a western bellcote, a complete set of contemporary plastered wagon roofs and a plastered vault to the seventeenth-century south porch. The church was restored by R. K. Penson in 1874 and again by C. W. Mercer in 1926. The fittings, including the pulpit, pews and altar rails are mostly by Penson. Early nineteenth-century fittings include some coloured glass, stone panels inscribed with the Ten Commandments, Creed and Lord's Prayer, the Holford of Cilgwyn hatchment and the painted Words of Institution to the north of the altar. There are several good eighteenth- and nineteenth-century memorial tablets, the best being one to Erasmus Williams who died in 1785.

NY

240. NEVERN/NANHYFER (St Brynach), Church in Wales *Pembs*

Location: off the B4582, 2 miles north-east of Newport (Pembrokeshire). *Access*: generally open.

One of the outstanding medieval sites of Wales. The church is in an oval churchyard, edged by a stream on the west side, and so heavily set with yew trees that on entering one seems to pass through darkness into light. Outside the church are two important early monuments. One, now barely legible, a fifth-/sixth-century ECM inscribed in two lines in Latin: 'VITALIANI EMERETO'; corresponding Ogham inscription around the edge: 'VITALIANI'. The other monument is a high cross of similar type to the early eleventh-century high cross at Carew, and presumably of similar date. The ornament is geometric, in four panels on each of the front, back and sides; inscriptions in cartouches on front and back: 'HAENH' (meaning unknown) and 'DNS' (*Dominus*). The cross-head is separate to the shaft.

The fabric of the church is probably mostly late medieval. A heavy, squat tower and broad nave with north and south chapels; the south chapel (probably fifteenth century) with turret stair and a loft. The chancel exits the nave on a distinct angle. The long narrow chancel with timberwork and colourful tiling makes a contrast with the rather plain nave. The church was heavily restored by Robert Jewell Withers in the nineteenth century, with most windows and chancel fittings dating from his restoration. The medieval font is twelfth century. A nice touch in the nave is kneelers decorated in a range of motifs from insular art. In the window sill of the south chapel are two stones. One is a slab with cross in relief, of indeterminate date. The other is a fifth-/sixth-century ECM with the Latin 'MAGLOCUNI FILI CLVTORI' ('[the stone] of Maglocunus [Maelgwn] son of Clutorus') and the equivalent in Ogham 'MAGLOCUNI

MAQI CLUTA[RI]'. The church at Nevern is an outstanding complex of medieval building, monuments and trees.

JW

241. NICHOLASTON (St Nicholas), Church in Wales   *Swan.*

Location: by itself beside the A4118, the south coast road in Gower, 2 miles west of Parkmill.
Access: key held at Parsonage Farm opposite the church.

The church, overlooking the centre of Oxwich bay, was almost wholly rebuilt in 1893–4 by G. E. Halliday in a most remarkable fashion. Funds for the rebuilding came from Miss Olive Talbot of the Mansel Talbot family who had owned Oxwich and Penrice since the Middle Ages, and had more recently become extremely wealthy by exploiting their estate at Margam for industrial purposes.

The diminutive church, rebuilt on its old foundations, retains its twelfth-century chancel arch. The new walls are of rough conglomerate, laid rock faced and coloured from grey to white to pink to blood red. In contrast, all the dressings are of the smoothest grey-green Quarella ashlar which has weathered the winds and rains of a century with no more blemish than abundant lichen growth. This is more remarkable because there are carvings everywhere, human and vegetable, on corbels, copings and capitals. The style is Early English, and the carver was William Clarke of Llandaff. Inside there is much more: the pulpit, reredos and vestry doorway (inspired by the prior's doorway at Norwich Cathedral) all loaded with figure carving.

JN

242. OXWICH (St Illtyd), Church in Wales   *Swan.*

Location: on the west side of Oxwich Bay approached by a narrow side road from the A4118, 3 miles south-west of Nicholaston.
Access: Sunday service at 9.45 a.m.

St Illtyd's is a small Norman two-cell church, with extensions to both chancel and nave in the fourteenth century. Especially notable is the narrow chancel arch, a rare survival. The church is entered through the battlemented tower at the western end. A niche in the nave known as 'Doolamur's Hole' contains fine effigies claimed to be of two members of the De La Mere family of Oxwich Castle, but this is disputed and the style of the figures may be fifteenth century. The church was rebuilt in 1892, at the instigation of the Talbots of Penrice, who also rebuilt Nicholaston.

JW

243. PEMBREY/PENBRE (St Illtyd), Church in Wales   *Carms*

Location: in the old part of the village, on the A484, 4 miles south-east of Kidwelly.
Access: details of key holders on notice board.

A large, thirteenth- to sixteenth-century, double-naved church, with a north-west tower and south-west double bellcote. It was restored by James Wilson of Bath in 1856–7 and by W. D. Caröe in 1910–11. Apart from the chancel, the rest of the church preserves a fine set of sixteenth-century roofs. At the east end of the nave are the remains of a former chantry chapel, including parts of a reredos, a tomb niche and a window recess with elaborately carved shields and heraldic devices. The outer door of the south porch dates from 1717. Caröe designed the pulpit and choir stalls and there is an interesting modern set of neo-classical three-sided altar rails.

NY

244. RUDBAXTON (St Michael), Church in Wales   *Pembs*

Location: by itself off the A40, 4 miles north of Haverfordwest.
Access: generally open between April and September.

This late medieval church has an unusual ground plan, with a short south aisle to the east of the south porch. The west tower was attractively lime rendered in 2001. The church was restored by Ewan Christian in 1845 and again by R. G. Pinder in 1892, and most furnishings date from this second restoration, apart from Christian's pews, from which the doors have been removed, in the south aisle, and the early nineteenth-century Gothick altar rails. At the east end of the south aisle is a magnificent late seventeenth-century painted monument to several members of the Howard family of Hetherhill.

NY

245. ST CLEARS/SANCLER (St Mary Magdalen), Church in Wales
Carms

Location: set back from the main road on the approach to the town from Laugharne.
Access: details of key holders on notice board.

A former priory church founded *c.*1100. The twelfth-century nave preserves its original font and splendid arch of three orders leading into the fifteenth-century chancel. The west tower, through which the church is entered, dates from the sixteenth century. The nave was restored by R. K. Penson in 1853–5 and the chancel by John Middleton in 1883–4. The pews, some of which have retained their doors, and the pulpit are Penson's. Over the chancel arch is an effective modern rood beam and figures.

NY

246. ST DAVIDS (St Davids Cathedral), Church in Wales   *Pembs*

Location: in city centre.
Access: generally open.

The most historic and architecturally significant of the cathedrals of Wales, St Davids Cathedral is one of the last great Romanesque buildings to be built in medieval Britain. The cathedral is the latest of a series of churches on the same site, probably stretching back to that of St David himself. The inconspicuous location of the cathedral, on somewhat unstable ground at the bottom of a valley, doubtless reflects the monastic origins of the site in the Early Middle Ages. The present building was commenced under the episcopacy of Peter de Leia in 1182, replacing an earlier structure, dedicated to St Andrew, which had been built by Bishop Bernard (1115–48), the first Norman appointment to the see. The chapel of St Thomas, which opens from the north transept, is at around two degrees variance from the alignment of the main building and this very likely reflects the alignment of the earlier cathedral – the shift no doubt being to accommodate the greater length of the present structure. The building today largely represents the plan of 1182 and the bulk of the visible masonry is medieval work, though with extensive replacement of individual stones. The crossing tower collapsed in 1220 and in 1248 an 'earthquake' (which may have been simply subsidence) caused further damage. These events along with many subsequent attempts at restoration account for the intricacy of the building one sees today.

The exterior was once lime rendered – of which traces are still visible – but is now exposed as a mixture of types of stone. The insipid west front is modern; the work of Sir George Gilbert Scott, replacing an earlier effort by Nash (some elements of which are still visible from inside the cathedral). The College of St Mary (now a cafe) and its restored cloister abuts the cathedral on the north side. It was founded by Bishop Adam Houghton (1361–89) and dissolved in 1549.

The interior of the cathedral presents a beautiful but sometimes bewildering puzzle of ornately decorated walls and ceiling. The nave slopes gently up to the crossing, where there are steps up to doors into the aisle-less transepts which flank the choir. The aisled presbytery is backed by the original east wall; the retrochoir and Lady chapel are later additions and the blocked lancets of the original east window are visible in the wall. The range of interior decoration is a mark of the importance of the cult of St David in the Middle Ages. The nave is in six bays with round arches in three orders. There is a wide variety of decoration on the arches and capitals. The pillars alternate between round and octagonal and the ornament on the second order of the arches changes from bay to bay, as it also does on the clerestory arches. The round arches of the nave contrast with the pointed arches of the tower and presbytery, which are likely to have been rebuilt after the collapse of 1220. The arches of the nave have rotated outward, perhaps as a result of the 1248 earthquake, and present a somewhat disconcerting aspect. Springers and piers on both the nave and aisle walls (and chiselling of the clerestory windows) indicate that a masonry vault was at least partially completed, and probably destroyed in 1248. The chancel has similar evidence of vaulting. The nave and presbytery are now roofed by magnificent timber ceilings. The suspended wooden ceiling of sixteenth-century date is the crowning glory of the nave. The suspended rood is by W. D. Caröe (1931).

Highlights of the cathedral include the pulpitum, a magnificent example of Decorated work, built by Bishop Henry de Gower (1328–47); it also contains de Gower's tomb. Gower also built the Bishop's Palace, also a magnificent example of Decorated. In one of the north bays of the presbytery is a shrine erected (1274–5) for the 'relics' of St David. The fan-vaulted Trinity Chapel (c.1520), now containing the reliquary of St David (the relics were recently dated to c.1000–1200), is outstanding. Medieval tombs around the aisles of the presbytery putatively include those of Gerald of Wales and Rhys ap Gruffydd (the Lord Rhys of Deheubarth). In the centre of the presbytery is the marble tomb of Edmund Tudor (d.1456), father of Henry VII, which was translated from Greyfriars in Carmarthen and placed in the centre of the choir as a very obvious political statement in the 1540s. The tomb of Countess Maidstone in the south aisle of the retrochoir is a somewhat overpowering work in alabaster with life-size effigy and inscription in Greek from the Book of Revelation. The cathedral contains work of major architects and designers of the nineteenth and twentieth centuries, including George Gilbert Scott, his son John Oldrid and William Butterfield as well as stained glass by Hardman and Kempe & Co.

JW

247. SWANSEA/ABERTAWE (St Mary), Church in Wales   *Swan.*

Location: in city centre.
Access: open daily, 9.30 a.m.–4 p.m.

The nave of the medieval church was rebuilt in 1739 and the whole building in 1894–8. It was gutted in 1941 and is one of the few Welsh churches that were rebuilt after the war. The very pedestrian design, working within the confines of the previous ground plan, was undertaken by L. T. Moore and Sir Percy Thomas, and supervised by the latter between

1954 and 1959. Despite this there are some good modern furnishings: the painting of the Deposition of Christ (1958) by Ceri Richards, stained glass in the Lady Chapel (1965–6) by John Piper and Patrick Reyntiens and the wrought-iron font canopy (1972) by George Pace.

NY

248. SWANSEA/ABERTAWE (New Shiloh/Siloh Newydd), Independent
Swan.

Location: in Landore, near the new Liberty Stadium, Siloh Road leaves the old main road (running parallel to the new dual carriageway leading north from the city centre towards the M4) just under the Landore railway viaduct; at the top of the hill the chapel is prominently sited at the junction of Siloh Road and Pentre Treharne.
Access: side door open on Fridays, 9 a.m.–10.30 a.m.

A very large chapel built by Thomas Freeman of Brynhyfryd (a prominent builder and Congregationalist) in 1876–7 – the 'New Siloh' of the name arises because it replaced the Old Siloh (which still survives as a secular building) at the bottom end of the road. It is of a rock-faced Pennant sandstone with a great deal of Bath stone enrichment, and in an idiosyncratic Lombardic style with only a few nods to classicism. It has an unusual five-bay façade, because the three central (round-headed) windows are divided only by thin colonnettes, above which is a huge half-round window, and below there is a three-gabled doorway enriched with much carving. Both sides of these doors are two long windows, and the façade is topped by a pediment which has at its peak what appears to be a four-armed cross, almost like a weathervane. The side elevations are of seven bays, with round-headed windows divided by pilasters. It has a large galleried interior, with an organ contained in a projection at the back with stained-glass windows on both sides. The chapel was for long celebrated for its choir and its concerts. The 'Ysgoldy' or schoolroom is on the east side a storey below, as Siloh Road falls away to the east, and has an unusual six-bay side elevation with three dormers above the rather idiosyncratic windows.

PM

249. SWANSEA/ABERTAWE (Mount Pleasant), Baptist *Swan.*

Location: in city centre.
Access: services on Sundays at 11 a.m and 6 p.m.

This splendid Bath-stone classical chapel, designed by George Morgan of Carmarthen in 1874–6 (on the site of an earlier chapel of 1825–6), dominates the east end of The Kingsway. It stands in a small yard with two trees to give contrast to the mass of the building, which is of five bays, the centre three fronted by four Corinthian columns supporting a pediment. The five doors and five windows are round headed, and there are pairs of Corinthian pilasters at both ends, completing a most satisfying composition. The side elevations are stuccoed, and set back discreetly several bays are a two-storey schoolroom (east side) and a lecture hall (west side), the former added in 1884, the latter in 1904–5.

The interior has galleries running around three sides of the chapel, set upon cast-iron columns and Doric entablatures, while above the pulpit the organ is recessed in a large archway in the shape of a Venetian window subdivided by Doric columns.

PM

250. TENBY/DINBYCH-Y-PYSGOD (St Mary), Church in Wales *Pembs*

Location: in town centre.
Access: generally open.

One of the largest and finest parish churches in Wales, dating mostly from the fourteenth and fifteenth centuries. It comprises an aisled nave, chancel with north and south chapels, south porch and a tower with a spire to the south-west of the chancel. The main restoration was by David Brandon in 1855–63 and there were later ones by J. P. Seddon in 1884 and by A. D. R. Caröe in 1960. The chancel is raised over a crypt and both the nave and the chancel have handsome fifteenth-century roofs. The large collection of medieval and early modern monuments include two elaborate altar tombs to Thomas White (d.1482) and his son John (d.1507); both were rich merchants and mayors of Tenby. The pulpit dates from 1634. The altar table, designed by J. L. Pearson and made in 1878, incorporates a fifteenth-century *mensa*.

NY

Guide to Further Reading

Bassett, T. M., *The Welsh Baptists* (Swansea, 1977).

Beazley, Elizabeth and Peter Howell, *The Companion Guide to North Wales* (London, 1975).

Davies, J. L. and C. Arnold, *Roman and Early Medieval Wales* (Stroud, 2000).

Davies, R. R., *Wales: The Age of Conquest, 1063–1415* (Oxford, 1987).

Davies, Wendy, *Wales in the Early Middle Ages* (Leicester, 1982).

Edwards, N. and A. Lane, *The Early Church in Wales and the West* (Oxford, 1992).

Haslam, Richard, *Buildings of Wales: Powys* (Harmondsworth, 1979).

——, Julian Orbach and Adam Voelcker, *Buildings of Wales: Gwynedd* (New Haven and London, 2009).

Howell, Peter and Elizabeth Beazley, *The Companion Guide to South Wales* (London, 1977).

Hubbard, Edward, *Buildings of Wales: Clwyd* (Harmondsworth, 1986).

Hughes, H. H. and H. L. North, *The Old Churches of Snowdonia* (London, 1924).

Jeffrey, Paul, *The Collegiate Churches of England and Wales* (London, 2004).

Jones, Anthony, *Welsh Chapels* (Stroud, 1996).

Jones, Francis, *The Holy Wells of Wales* (Cardiff, 1954).

Jones, H. Wyn, *Pocket Guide to the Place-Names of Wales* (Cardiff, 2000).

Jones, R. T., *Congregationalism in Wales* (Cardiff, 2004).

Leask, H. G., *Irish Churches and Monastic Buildings*, vol. 1, *The First Phases and the Romanesque* (Dundalk, 1955).

Lloyd, Thomas, Julian Orbach and Robert Scourfield, *Buildings of Wales: Carmarthenshire and Ceredigion* (New Haven and London, 2006).

——, *Buildings of Wales: Pembrokeshire* (New Haven and London, 2004).

Lord, Peter, *The Visual Culture of Wales: Medieval Vision* (Cardiff, 2003).

Morgan, D. L., *The Great Awakening in Wales* (London, 1988).

Newman, John, *Buildings of Wales: Gwent* (London, 2000).

——, *Buildings of Wales: Glamorgan* (London, 1995).

Owen, D. H., *Capeli Cymru* (Talybont, 2005).

Petts, D., *The Early Medieval Church in Wales* (Stroud, 2009).

Redknap, M., J. Lewis and Nancy Edwards, *A Corpus of Early Medieval Inscribed Stones and Stone Sculpture in Wales*, 2 vols (Cardiff, 2007).

Thurlby, M., *Romanesque Architecture and Sculpture in Wales* (Logaston, 2006).

——, William Jacob, Nigel Yates and Frances Knight, *The Welsh Church from Reformation to Disestablishment, 1603–1920* (Cardiff, 2007).

——, *Wales and the Reformation* (Cardiff, 1999).

——, *The Welsh Church from Conquest to Reformation* (Cardiff, 1962).

Yates, Nigel, *Buildings, Faith and Worship: The Liturgical Arrangement of Anglican Churches 1600–1900* (Oxford, 2000).

Glossary

abbey	a house of monks ruled by its own abbot
abbot	the head of a community of monks that is self-governing
aisle	side area, subsidiary to the main church, usually separated from it by arches
almsbox	box in the church for the collection of money for the poor, or for the church
altar rails	rails dividing the sanctuary (q.v.) from the rest of the building
altar table	a wooden table at which the Holy Communion is celebrated in an Anglican church
angelus bell	bell rung for the triple Hail Mary
An Túr Gloine (the glass tower)	Irish Arts and Crafts company, founded in 1903 by Sarah Purser and Edward Martyn
apse	semicircular space covered by hemispherical vault, usually at the rear of the chancel
apsidal	a space shaped similarly to an apse, for example, a chapel
arcade	a row of arches supported by piers
archdeacon	a senior clergyman responsible for a territorial pastorate encompassing many parishes
Arminian	a group within the Anglican and Calvinist churches which rejected the orthodox Calvinist doctrines of predestination and election
Arts and Crafts movement	decorative arts movement of the late nineteenth century, which placed an emphasis on craftsmanship rather than mass-production; closely linked to the Pre-Raphaelite movement (q.v.)

ashlar	dressed stone used in masonry
Augustinian Canons	an order of religious canons following the Rule of St Augustine of Hippo
Baptist	Protestant denomination characterised by its rejection of infant baptism and belief in adult baptism by immersion
barrel roof (also wagon roof)	ceiling of densely packed arches making one more or less continuous vault
batter	outward turn of a wall towards the base of a building
bay	division of internal space defined by an arch
bellcote	roof-level structure, often a simple arch, to house church bells
Benedicite	canticle of three children in the fiery furnace, from the Book of Daniel
Benedictine	order of monks following the Rule of St Benedict; the Benedictine tradition included not only the Benedictine order, but orders such as the Cistercians, Cluniacs and Tironians, who followed the same rule and are known generally as 'reformed Benedictines'
benefaction boards	panels in churches recording gifts to the poor and other charitable bequests
bishop	consecrated and ordained leading clergyman who normally rules over a territorial diocese
bosses	knobs or similar projections
box pews	pews with doors, often with seats on three sides, popular in churches and chapels before c.1850
broach spire	an octagonal spire that sits on a square tower
buttress	supporting structure projecting from wall to counteract lateral thrust; also see flying buttresses (q.v.)
Calvinist	churches tracing their origins to the ideas of John Calvin; also known as the 'Reformed Tradition'

Calvinistic Methodist	also known as 'Presbyterian Church of Wales'; Protestant denomination that rose out of eighteenth-century Methodism under figures such as Howell Harris and Daniel Rowland; the Calvinistic Methodist tradition has produced a large number of the most famous hymns in the Welsh language
cancelli	low screen separating the chancel from the nave
candelabrum(-a)	candlestick that branches from a single stem into several places for candles
cantref	medieval Welsh territorial division
capel y bedd	chapel with a founder's or saint's grave
ceilure	decorated ceiling in chancel
cell	variously: a room of a church building (hence 'single-cell', etc.), a monastic hut or a subsidiary foundation of a larger, usually monastic, church; place-name element found in names such as Dolgellau, Cellan
chamfer	to cut off a corner to form a new surface
chancel	the eastern part of a church containing the main altar
chancel arch	arch separating the nave from the chancel
chantry chapel	chapel within a church dedicated to a benefactor or family thereof
chapel	in Catholic (including Anglican) usage, a minor church building or subsidiary part of a church; in Nonconformist tradition the building used for services
church	in the Catholic tradition (including Anglican) generally used for both the denomination as a whole and the buildings used for worship; in the Nonconformist tradition often used to describe the people but not the buildings of the church; hence in Wales 'church' colloquially used to describe Anglicans, 'chapel' to describe

	Nonconformists, distinguishing them by the buildings in which they worship
Cistercian	reformed Benedictine monastic order founded at Citeaux in France in 1098; there were a large number of Cistercian houses in Wales
clas(-au)	medieval community of secular priests living under the headship of a titular abbot, who may himself be a priest or a layman
claswyr	clas + gwŷr = 'men of the clas'
clerestory	the storey of a church that extends above the roof of a side aisle, allowing for windows opening directly to the outside
Cluniac	reformed Benedictine monastic order founded at Cluny in France in 909
colidei	probably from Irish céli Dé ('client of God')/'culdee'; an extreme ascetic
collegiate church	a church housing a 'college' or community of priests or persons in minor orders
colonnettes	small columns/shafts
communion pew/ enclosure	large area, frequently including seating, within which the communion table is located in Nonconformist chapels
consistory court	diocesan court, presided over by the Chancellor, dealing with trial of clergy on certain matters, faculties (planning requests for Anglican churches) and, until 1857, marriage and probate matters
Corinthian columns	classical order of column with crockets on the capital
crockets	hooked-over leaves
cruciform	church laid out in the shape of a cross, i.e. with transepts
dado	decoration of the lower half of an interior wall
diocese	territory of the jurisdiction of a bishop

Dissenting	Protestant traditions that broke from the Church of England; generally used synonymously with 'Nonconformist', although the latter really only applies to those who broke after 1662
dog-tongs	extending metal tongs traditionally used to remove dogs from the church
Ecclesiologist	movement, beginning in the 1840s, to promote medieval style architecture, especially in interiors and liturgical arrangement
ECM	early Christian monument, the common term for an inscribed stone of the period c.400–1000 AD
elder	in some Protestant denominations denotes a minister or pastor, in others a senior lay member of the church
encaustic tiles	vitrified painted tile, characteristic of wealthy medieval churches and replicated in the nineteenth century
Evangelical revival	movement in the Anglican church, linked to the Wesleyan (q.v.) revival, which encouraged pietism in the Church of England and Protestant styles of worship
family pews	reserved pews in church, usually for gentry
fan-vaulted	ceiling vaults made of fine supports in fanned half-cones; characteristic of the Perpendicular style (q.v.)
finial	decorative moulding on the end of a gable or top of wall
flèche	slender spire in the centre of a roof
flying buttress	buttress (q.v.) made up of a half-arch standing out from the wall
font	basin, usually elevated, for the purpose of baptism
Gothic	decorative style common from the twelfth century onward, distinguished from the earlier Romanesque particularly by use of pointed

arches; phases of Gothic include Early English, French, Decorated and Perpendicular.

Gothick (or Neo-Gothic)	style that imitates medieval Gothic, usually only in general terms
Gregorian Reform	reform movement in the western church led by the papacy in the eleventh century; its ultimate effect was to make appointments to the church more independent of secular authorities than previously, as well as to encourage clerical celibacy
Grisaille glass	glass painted or etched in monochrome
ha-ha	sunken fence of ditch and stone facing designed not to interrupt the view across a site
half uncial	form of Latin script used in early medieval manuscripts
hammerbeam	timber roof truss, characterised by stepped braces on the interior
hearse house	carriage house in churchyard for storing a hearse
hipped roof	peaked roof, with ridge giving way at either end to sloping roof down to gutter level
hood-mould	external mould (or lip) to throw off rainwater over a window
Independent	Welsh union of Protestant churches founded in the seventeenth century
keeled decoration	rib decoration, usually on an arch, resembling a ship's keel
Lady chapel	chapel dedicated to the Virgin Mary, often the largest chapel of a cathedral
lancet	narrow window with pointed arch, characteristic of Gothic style
Laudian	after William Laud (archbishop of Canterbury 1633–45) and opponent of Puritanism, who instituted the removal of communion tables to behind altar rails
lectern	stand topped by a desk for the reading of a book

liturgical arrangement	arrangement of church for the performance of a specific liturgy
liturgy	the pattern of worship, usually following printed instructions, of a particular faith
loggia	corridor or portico, usually arcaded (q.v.), open to the air on one side
lychgate	roofed gate into a churchyard, associated with funerary ritual
Mabsant, or *Gŵyl Mabsant*	festival in which a Welsh congregation celebrated their local patron saint
meeting house	another term for an early Nonconformist chapel
mensa (Lat. 'table')	flat surface of the top of the altar
Methodist	Dissenting tradition that originated as a movement in the Church of England advocating 'Methodistic' preaching and Protestant trends in worship. It later broke from the Church of England to form distinct denominations: Calvinist and Wesleyan. In modern usage 'Methodist' is mostly by itself used to denote Wesleyans, though in Wales Calvinistic Methodists are in the majority.
misericord	small shelf in a choir stall, used to sit upon during sung liturgy
monastic range	the extent of the main buildings of a monastery, forming a unit with the monastic church
narthex	entry area or lobby, usually at the outer end of the nave
nave	usually the largest part of a church building, in which the main congregation worships; usually at the opposite (commonly western) end to the chancel, but may be a separate room to the chancel, or simply one end of the same room
Nonconformity	see Dissenting
Ogham script	an Irish cipher made up of straight lines in clusters, used on monuments of the fifth and

	sixth centuries AD, especially in Pembrokeshire
orders	variously: in architecture, the successive arches constituting a Romanesque arch or doorway, or the classical orders of decoration (e.g. Corinthian); types of monasticism (e.g. Augustinian Order); distinct from 'ordering', which in an ecclesiastical context is used to mean arrangement of furniture for liturgical practice
organ screen	screen, especially in cathedrals, on which the organ is placed
Oxford Movement	movement in the Anglican church, starting in the 1830s, promoting a more Catholic vision of the church; early proponents were John Keble and John Henry Newman; also see Tractarians
parish chest	chest in which the parish's documents and communion plate were stored
parish room	free-standing building, often in the churchyard, used for social events or parochial meetings
parclose	screen or rail enclosing a side chapel or tomb
pediment	decorated space on gable end or in triangle over window, etc.
Perpendicular	late development of Gothic style, prominent in the fourteenth to sixteenth centuries
piscina	basin for the washing of liturgical vessel, usually an inset in the wall with a drain in the bottom
Plygain	Christmas singing service at dawn (lit. 'cockcrow')
polychrome	style involving the use of multiple colours, common in the nineteenth century
Pre-Raphaelite	aesthetic movement of the nineteenth century, closely linked to the Arts and Crafts movement; leading figures were Dante Gabriel Rosetti and William Morris

Prebendary	A prebendal church is one for which an incumbent was appointed from a central chapter associated with a larger foundation such as a cathedral.
Presbyterian Church of Wales	see Calvinistic Methodist
priory	a house of monks or religious canons headed by prior, dependent on a mother abbey (if the latter abroad, in which case often termed an 'alien priory')
proprietary churches	a church built on private land, usually by a private individual who retained rights of appointment of clergy
Protestant	churches formed on the basis of, or deriving inspiration from, the Protestant Reformation in the sixteenth century
pulpit	raised enclosed platform, from which the priest preaches the sermon.
Quaker	'The Religious Society of Friends', independently formed Nonconformist group that emerged in the seventeenth century
reading desk	desk from which an Anglican clergyman read the service and the lessons, but not used for preaching
rebus	coded heraldic symbol, usually making a pun on the name of the owner
reredos	decorated screen behind the altar
retrochoir	area behind the high altar of a church
ritualism	development of Anglo-Catholicism around the end of the nineteenth century, which sought to introduce more Catholic liturgical practices into the Church of England
rood beam/loft/ screen/stair	crucifix flanked by Virgin Mary and St John, commonly at the entrance to the chancel; the

	rood was often on a rood beam, with a screen underneath and a loft above, reached by a stair
sconces	upward pointing light fixture, fastened to wall as its support
Second Vatican Council (or Vatican II)	The Second Ecumenical Council of the Catholic Church (1962–5); the council made wide-ranging changes to Catholic liturgy and practice, many of which had an impact on practices in other churches as well
secular canon	priest attached to a central church
sedilia (pl. of Lat. *sedile* 'seat')	seats, usually on the south (generally right-hand) side of the chancel, on which sat the priest, deacon and sub-deacon; often an arcaded niche
sêt-fawr	seating on which the elders or deacons of a Protestant chapel sat, facing either the congregation or the pulpit
shaft ring	ring of stone encircling a shaft at a junction point
side altar	subsidiary altar in Anglican or Roman Catholic churches
single cell	a church or chapel of one room
spirelet	see *flèche*
squint	a niche cut in the wall of the church to allow a person to view the altar
stalls	benches, usually divided, for the individual seating of a choir or the clergy
stoup	a vessel for holding holy water, often at the door of a church
Sunday schoolroom	separate hall for Sunday school classes in a Protestant chapel complex
surpliced choir	choir wearing white, knee-length vestments
synod	a council of bishops
tester	hanging canopy over a pulpit, tomb or altar
three-decker pulpit	a pulpit with reading desk and clerk's desk below

Tractarian	branch of the Oxford Movement (see above), which produced a series of theological texts known as 'Tracts for the Times'. Tractarian churches reflect the distinct principles of Anglo-Catholic liturgy.
transepts	structures, usually equal in height with the nave, extending at right angles from a 'crossing' between chancel and nave, to make a 'cruciform' church
triforium	storey above the level of ground floor, sometimes separate to clerestory, sometimes incorporating it
truss	a timber structure supporting a roof
twin cell	two-roomed church
tympanum	area bounded by lintel and arch above a door, usually semicircular
Unitarian	group that emerged in the eighteenth century and which rejected the doctrine of the Trinity (that God is three persons: Father, Son and Holy Spirit). Unitarianism had considerable popularity in parts of Wales, especially the Teifi valley
Vatican II	see Second Vatican Council
vaults	arches supporting a stone roof
vicar	in the Anglican tradition historically the holder of a parish receiving only lesser tithes (tithes are now abolished), as distinct from a rector. Now often used generally to simply mean parish priest, though many parishes still maintain the distinction in terminology. In Catholic tradition used literally to mean a person acting as the agent of another, hence the pope is the 'Vicar of Christ'
Wesleyan	churches tracing their origins to the Methodist John Wesley; see also Methodism

Churches and Chapels

Index

Montgomery/Trefaldwyn, *Powys* 9, 46
Morgan, George (1834–1915),
    architect 116, 171, 191
Morris (William, 1834–96) & Co.,
    stained-glass makers 80, 91, 116,
    117, 122
Morriston, *Swan.* 182–3
Mostyn family of Llandudno 57, 87
Moxham, Egbert (1822–64), architect
    143
Mountain Ash, Rhondda 134
Mwnt, *Cere.* 47
Myddfai, *Carms* 183
Myddleton, Mary, of Wrexham 74
Myddleton, Richard (d.1575),
    governor of Denbigh Castle 58
Myers, George (1805–75), sculptor 67

Nanhoron, *Gwyn.* 108
Nash, *Newpt* 160
Nash, John (1752–1835), architect 188
Naylor, Georgina, of Leighton 29
Neath 21
Nesfield, William Eden (1835–88),
    architect 63
Nevern/Nanhyfer, *Pembs* 183
Newbery, Robert J. (1861–1940),
    stained-glass maker 179
Newborough, third lord (Spencer
    Bulkeley Wynn, d.1888) 96
Newbridge/Cefnbychan, *Torfaen* 160
Newman, John Henry (1801–90),
    Cardinal 40
Newport/Casnewydd 161–2
Newport and Menevia, diocese of 15, 119
Newton Nottage, *Bridg.* 136
Nicholaston, *Swan.* 184, 186
Nollekens, Joseph (1737–1823),
    sculptor 96

North, Herbert Luck (1871–1941),
    architect 113
Norton, John (1823–1904), architect
    19, 135, 157

Oates, John (1793–1831), architect
    55
Oakley, Mrs W. E. of Plas Tan-y-Bwlch
    108
O'Connor, Michael (1801–67) and
    Arthur (1826–73), stained-glass
    makers 55, 89
Ogham stones 2, 7, 169, 174, 184
Old Radnor/Pencraig, *Powys* 9, 48
Olsen, Roy, architect 88
Ould, Edward Augustus Lyle
    (1852–1909), architect 60
Overbeck, Johann Friedrich
    (1789–1869), artist 68
Owen, Revd Benjamin, Merthyr Tydfil
    134
Owen, John, bishop of St Davids
    (1897–1926) 14
Oxwich, *Swan.* 132, 184–6

Pace, George G. (1915–75), architect
    20, 23, 117, 127–8, 156, 190
Padarn, St 30, 34
Palé Hall 95
Paley and Austin of Lancaster,
    architects 80, 107
Pantasaph, *Flint.* 67
Parker, John Henry (1801–84),
    antiquary 41
Parsons, Revd Charles 137
Partrishow, *Powys* 48
Pearson, John Loughborough
    (1817–97), architect 14, 32, 39,
    51, 68, 69, 140, 192
Pembrey/Penbre, *Carms* 185